13 20

MAKE YOUR OWN

KNITTED
TOYS

MAKE YOUR OWN
KNITTED
TOYS

MOLLY GODDARD

PHOTOGRAPHY BY JUAN ESPI

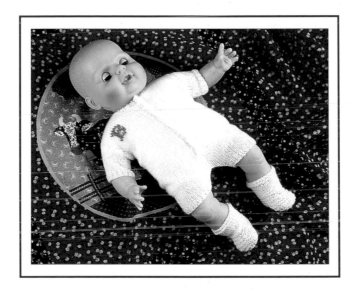

NEW
HOLLAND

First published in the UK in 1993 by
New Holland (Publishers) Ltd
37 Connaught Street, London W2 2AZ

ISBN 1 85368 255 1

Editor: Elizabeth Frost
Designer: Janice Evans
Assistant designer: Lauren Mendelson
Photographer: Juan Espi

Typeset by Lauren Mendelson
Reproduction by Unifoto (Pty) Ltd
Printed and bound in Singapore by Tien Wah Press (Pte) Ltd

CONTENTS

AUTHOR'S ACKNOWLEDGEMENTS

I would like to thank the following people for their help and support: Union Spinning Mills (Pty) Ltd for very kindly supplying all the yarns and polyester filling used for making the toys and dolls' clothes, and especially Bonnie Maré for always having confidence in me; Margaret de Wet and Sonja Hardie for helping me with the knitting; Michael Carr for coping with my bad handwriting and typing the manuscript; *Your Family* magazine for giving me permission to use two patterns already published; Linda de Villiers of Struik for persuading me to write the book, and my family for supporting me and living in chaos for a few months.

ABBREVIATIONS

alt	alternate	R(W)S	right (wrong) side	B	black
approx	approximate(ly)	rem	remain(ing)	BL	blue
beg	begin(ning)	rep	repeat(ed)	C	cream
ch	chain	rev	reverse(ing)	CH	charcoal
cont	continue	rev st st	reversed stocking	DB	dark brown
dc	double crochet		stitch	G	grey
dec	decrease(ing)	skpo	slip one, knit one,	GR	green
DK	double knitting		pass slipped stitch	L	lilac
end	end(ing)		over	LB	light brown (beige)
fol	follow(ing)	st st	stocking stitch	M	mauve
gst	garter stitch	st(s)	stitch(es)	PK	pink
inc	increase(ing)	tbl	through back of	R	red
k	knit		loop	W	white
N(s)	needle(s)	tog	together	Y	yellow
no.	number	yon	yarn over needle		
patt	pattern	yrn	yarn round needle		
p	purl	M1	make a stitch by		
R(L)HN	right- (left-) hand		lifting horizontal		
	needle		loop lying before		
			next st and working		
			into back of it		

INTRODUCTION

Welcome to the world of knitted toys, which are the easiest soft toys to make. All you need is a basic knowledge of knitting and a little patience when filling and stitching the toys together. I have deliberately chosen toys that are not difficult to make and have used polyester filling so that they are completely washable. I have used only felt for features where needed so they are safe for even the smallest baby. Feel free to use plastic noses and eyes instead if you wish.

The toys and clothes in this book have been made with pure acrylic double knitting (DK) or 4 ply yarn, unless otherwise stated. Any acrylic yarn of the same weight may be used.

The patterns have been written for work of average tension. However, the tension is not critical, and any variation will only make the toy a little larger or smaller. What is important, though, is that the knitting is firm enough to hold the filling, so if you tend to knit loosely, use thinner needles to compensate for your tension.

As far as possible, stitch the sections of the toys together on the wrong side and turn to the right side before filling, to achieve a neater finish. Unless otherwise instructed, fill firmly, but not too tightly, as this will stretch the knitting, resulting in an ugly finish. Use the blunt end of a knitting needle to ease the filling into difficult places. Where possible, do a double row of stitching around major joins like necks and limbs as this will be firmer and more secure.

I have not provided patterns for the felt features. Most of the eyes are round or oval, and the best way to make them is to cut the pieces a little larger than you would like them to be, pin them in place, and judge for yourself. Make mouths and other features from felt in the same way. Use satin stitch to embroider eyes or noses where necessary, and then work around the feature with stem stitch to give a neat finish.

Note: readers are advised to read a pattern from beginning to end before starting work on a toy.

LARRY LION

MATERIALS
100 g (4 oz) DK in light brown and a small ball of the same yarn in dark brown; one pair of 3.75 mm (No. 9) knitting needles; polyester filling; small pieces of felt in black and yellow for eyes.

LENGTH
Approx 28 cm (11 in).

ABBREVIATIONS
See page 7.

Note: entire lion is worked in gst.

LEGS (make 4)
Using LB, cast on 24 sts and k 8 rows.
Next row: K10, (k2tog) twice, k10.
K 1 row.
Next row: K9, (k2tog) twice, k9.
K 1 row.
Next row: K8, (k2tog) twice, k8.
(18 sts.)
K 16 rows.
Cast off.

BODY
Using LB, cast on 8 sts and k 1 row.
Next row: (Inc in next st) 8 times.
(16 sts.)
K 2 rows.
Next row: (K1, inc in next st) 8 times. (24 sts.)
K 2 rows.
Next row: (K1, inc in next st) 12 times. (36 sts.)
K 2 rows.
Next row: (K2, inc in next st) 12 times. (48 sts.)
K 44 rows.
Next row: (K2, k2tog) 12 times. (36 sts.)
K 2 rows.
Next row: (K1, k2tog) 12 times. (24 sts.)
K 2 rows.
Next row: (K2tog) 12 times. (12 sts.)
K 2 rows.
Next row: (K2tog) 6 times. (6 sts.)

K 1 row.
Cast off.

HEAD (make 2)
Using LB, cast on 10 sts and k 1 row.
Inc one st at each end of next row and fol 3 alt rows. (18 sts.)
K 16 rows. Place markers at each end of last row.
Dec 1 st at each end of next row and fol 3 alt rows. (10 sts.)
K 1 row.
Cast off.

HEAD GUSSET
Using LB, cast on 2 sts and k 1 row.
Next row: Inc in both sts.
Next 2 rows: Inc 1 st at each end.
Rep last 3 rows three times more. (12 sts.)
K 20 rows.
Next row: Dec 1 st at each end.
Next 2 rows: K to end.
Rep last 3 rows four times more. (2 sts.)
Next row: K2tog; fasten off.

SOLES (make 4)
Using LB, cast on 3 sts and k 1 row.
Inc 1 st at each end of next and fol alt row. (7 sts.)

K 6 rows.
Dec 1 st at each end of next row and fol alt row. (3 sts.)
K 1 row.
Cast off.

EARS (make 2)
Using LB, cast on 9 sts and k 10 rows.
Dec 1 st at each end of next 3 rows. (3 sts.)
Cast off.

TAIL
Using LB, cast on 5 sts and k 18 rows.
Cast off.

MANE
Using DB, cast on 61 sts and k 1 row.
Next row: * K1, k next st in the same way but do not slip it off LHN. Insert RHN into back of same st, wind yarn round first and second fingers at back of work, then complete st, slipping original st (now 2) off RHN. Yon and pass previous st(s) over the yon. Rep from * to last st, k1.
Rep last 2 rows three times more.
Cast off.

NOSE
Using DB, cast on 6 sts and k 8 rows.
Dec 1 st at each end of next row and fol alt row. (2 sts.)
Next row: K2tog; fasten off.

TO MAKE UP
Stitch sides of legs together and stitch soles in place. Fill. Stitch side edges of body, leaving a section open for filling. Fill and stitch closed. Stitch gusset to head pieces, beg and end at markers.
  Stitch rem sides tog, leaving cast-on edge open for filling. Fill and stitch firmly to body. Stitch legs to body.
  Stitch mane in place around head and stitch ears and nose in place. Embroider features and cut eyes from felt; slip-stitch in place.

TERENCE TIGER

MATERIALS
Approx 50 g (2 oz) each of yellow and black DK; one pair of 3.75 mm (No. 9) knitting needles; polyester filling; small pieces of felt in black and yellow for eyes.

HEIGHT
Approx. 28 cm (11 in).

ABBREVIATIONS
See page 7.

Note: entire tiger is worked in gst. Stripe pattern is used throughout, except on soles, ears and tail.

STRIPE PATTERN
K 2 rows Y.
K 2 rows B.
Rep these 4 rows for stripe patt.

LEGS (make 4)
Using Y, cast on 24 sts. K 8 rows.
Next row: K10, (k2tog) twice, k10.
K 1 row.
Next row: K9, (k2tog) twice, k9.
K 1 row.
Next row: K8, (k2tog) twice, k8.
(18 sts.)
K 16 rows.
Cast off.

BODY
Using Y, cast on 8 sts and k 1 row.
Next row: (Inc in next st) 8 times.
(16 sts.)
K 2 rows.
Next row: (K1, inc in next st) 8 times. (24 sts.)
K 2 rows.
Next row: (K1, inc in next st) 12 times. (36 sts.)
K 2 rows.
Next row: (K2, inc in next st) 12 times. (48 sts.)
K 44 rows.
Next row: (K2, k2tog) 12 times. (36 sts.)
K 2 rows.
Next row: (K1, k2tog) 12 times.

(24 sts.)
K 2 rows.
Next row: (K2tog) 12 times.
(12 sts.)
K 2 rows.
Next row: (K2tog) 6 times.
(6 sts.)
K 1 row. Cast off.

HEAD (make 2)
Using Y, cast on 10 sts and k 1 row.
Inc one st at each end of next row and fol 3 alt rows.
(18 sts.)
K 16 rows. Place markers at each end of last row.
Dec 1 st at each end of next row and fol 3 alt rows.
(10 sts.)
K 1 row.
Cast off.

HEAD GUSSET
Using Y, cast on 2 sts and k 1 row.
Next row: Inc in both sts.
K 2 rows.

Inc 1 st at each end of next row.
Rep last 3 rows three times more.
(12 sts.)
K 20 rows.
Next row: Dec 1 st at each end.
Next 2 rows: K to end.
Rep last 3 rows four times more.
(2 sts.)
Next row: K2tog; fasten off.

SOLES (make 4)
Using Y, cast on 3 sts and k 1 row.
Inc 1 st at each end of next row and fol alt row.
(7 sts.)
K 6 rows.
Dec 1 st at each end of next row and fol alt row.
(3 sts.)
K 1 row. Cast off.

EARS (make 2)
Using Y, cast on 9 sts and k 10 rows.
Dec 1 st at each end of next 3 rows.
(3 sts.) Cast off.

NOSE
Using B, cast on 6 sts and k 8 rows.
Dec 1 st at each end of next row and fol alt row.
(2 sts.)
Next row: K2tog; fasten off.

TAIL
Using Y, cast on 5 sts and k 18 rows.
Cast off.

TO MAKE UP
Stitch sides of legs together and stitch soles in place. Fill. Stitch side edges of body, leaving a section open for filling. Fill and stitch closed. Stitch head gusset to head pieces, beg and end at markers. Stitch rem sides tog, leaving cast-on edge open for filling. Fill and stitch firmly to body. Stitch legs to body. Fold tail in half, stitch side seams and stitch to body. Make a small fringe from B and attach to tail. Stitch ears and nose in place. Embroider mouth and cut eyes from felt; slip-stitch in place. Make whiskers from B.

HARRIET HIPPO

MATERIALS
Approx 100 g (4 oz) of DK in grey and a small ball of the same yarn in pink; one pair of 3.75 mm (No. 9) knitting needles; polyester filling; 1 m (1 yd) ribbon; small pieces of felt in black for features.

LENGTH
Approx 32 cm (12½ in).

ABBREVIATIONS
See page 7.

Note: entire hippo is worked in grey, except for the inner ears, and in st st.

BODY (make 2)
Cast on 14 sts and k 1 row.
Cont in st st and cast on 3 sts at beg of next 6 rows. (32 sts.)
Work 39 rows st st, beg with p row.
Cast off 3 sts at beg of next 4 rows. (20 sts.)
Cast off.

HEAD (make 2)
Cast on 10 sts and k 1 row.
Cont in st st and cast on 3 sts at beg of next 6 rows. (28 sts.)
Work 21 rows st st, beg with p row.
Cast off 2 sts at beg of next 4 rows. (20 sts.)
Cast off.

LEGS (make 4)
Cast on 14 sts.
Next row: K, inc in each st. (28 sts.)
Work 12 rows st st, beg with p row.
Next row: * P2tog, rep from * to end. (14 sts.)
Cast off.

SOLES (make 4)
Cast on 5 sts and work 2 rows st st.
Next row: K, inc one st at each end. (7 sts.)
Work 3 rows st st, beg with p row.
Next row: K, dec 1 st at each end. (5 sts.)
P 1 row. Cast off.

EARS (make 2 G and 2 PK)
Cast on 8 sts and work 8 rows st st.
Dec 1 st at each end of next row and fol 2 alt rows.
Next row: P2tog; fasten off.

TAIL
Cast on 6 sts and work 12 rows st st.
Thread yarn through sts, draw tog, and fasten off.

EYES (make 2)
Cast on 7 sts and work 2 rows st st.
Next row: K, inc 1 st at each end. (9 sts.)
Work 3 rows st st, beg with p row.
Next row: K, dec one st at each end. (7 sts.)

P 1 row.
Cast off.

TO MAKE UP
Stitch body sections tog, leaving cast-off edges open for neck. Fill. Stitch head sections tog, leaving cast-off edges open for neck. Fill and stitch to body. Stitch side seams of legs, stitch soles to cast-on edges and fill. Stitch to body. Stitch ears tog in pairs and stitch to head. Tie bow around neck. Run gathering thread around edges of eyes and draw up to form a ball. Fill lightly and stitch to head.

Cut features from felt and stitch in place.

GEORGE GIRAFFE

HEIGHT
Approx 30 cm (12 in).

ABBREVIATIONS
See page 7.

BODY AND LEGS
Begin at back leg
* Using Y, cast on 12 sts and work 16 rows st st.*
Break off yarn and leave sts on a spare N.
Work front leg and body
Work as for back from * to *.
Next row: K12, cast on 14, k across 12 sts for back leg. (38 sts.) **
Next 5 rows: Work in st st, beg with p row.
Next row: K to last st, inc in last st.
Rep last 6 rows twice more. (41 sts.)
Work 5 rows st st, beg with p row.
Shape back and neck
Next row: Cast off 7 sts, k to last st, inc in last st.
P 1 row.
Next row: Cast off 7 sts, k to end.
Next row: P to end.
Rep last 2 rows once more. (21 sts.)
Next row: Cast off 7 sts, k to last st, inc in last st. (15 sts.)
P 1 row.
Work 2 rows st st.
Next row: K2tog, k to end.
Next row: P to end.
Rep last 2 rows once more. (13 sts.)
Next row: K2tog, k to last st, inc in last st.
Work 3 rows st st, beg with p row.
Next row: K2tog, k to end.
Next row: P to end.

Rep last 6 rows once more. (11 sts.)
K 1 row.
Next row: Cast on 3 sts, p to end.
Work 7 rows st st.
Next row: Cast off 4 sts, p to end. (10 sts.)
K 1 row.
Dec 1 st at each end of next 3 rows. (4 sts.)
Cast off.
Work another side to match this one, rev all shapings.

UNDERBODY (make 2)
Work as for body to **.
Work 7 rows st st, beg with p row.
Cast off.

HEAD GUSSET
Using Y, cast on 2 sts and work 2 rows st st.
Next row: Inc in both sts.
Work 5 rows st st, beg with p row.
Next row: (K2tog) twice.
Next row: P2tog; fasten off.

EARS (make 2)
Using Y, cast on 4 sts and k 6 rows.
K 2 rows, dec 1 st at each end of each row.
Next row: K2tog; fasten off.

HORNS (make 2)
Using B, cast on 4 sts and k 6 rows.
Cast off.

TAIL
Using B, cast on 6 sts and k 20 rows.
Cast off.

HOOVES (make 4)
Using B, cast on 4 sts and k 1 row.
Next row: K, inc 1 st at each end.
K 4 rows.
Next row: K, dec 1 st at each end.
Cast off.

TO MAKE UP
Stitch cast-off edges of two underbody pieces together. Stitch sides of underbody legs to relevant sides of body legs. Stitch hooves in place. Stitch rem body seams, leaving top of head open for gusset and a section open at back for filling. Stitch head gusset in place and fill firmly. Stitch ears in place. Fold horns in half, stitch side seams and stitch to head. Fold tail in half, stitch side seam and stitch to body. Make a small fringe from B and attach to tail. Embroider features, and spots, using duplicate stitch.

ZOLLY ZEBRA

MATERIALS

Approx 50 g (2 oz) each of DK in black and white; one pair 3.75 mm (No. 9) knitting needles; polyester filling; small pieces of felt in black and white for eyes.

LENGTH

Approx 28 cm (11 in).

ABBREVIATIONS

See page 7.

Note: entire zebra is worked in st st and all sections, except tail, hooves and ears, are worked in stripe patt.

STRIPE PATT

Work 2 rows st st using B.
Work 2 rows st st using W.
Rep these 4 rows for stripe patt.

BODY

Using B, cast on 12 sts and work 2 rows.
Inc one st at each end of next row and fol 4 alt rows. (22 sts.)
Work 29 rows st st without shaping, beg with p row. Place marker at end of last row.
Shape neck
Next row: Cast off 2 sts, k to last 2 sts, k2tog.
Next row: P to end.
Rep last 2 rows twice more. (13 sts.)
Cast off.
Work another side to match this one, rev neck shapings.

BODY GUSSET

Using B, cast on 3 sts and work 2 rows.
Inc one st at each end of next row and fol 3 alt rows. (11 sts.)
Work 27 rows st st, beg with p row.
Dec one st at each end of next row and fol 3 alt rows. (3 sts.)
P 1 row. Cast off.

HEAD

Using B, cast on 7 sts; work 2 rows.

Inc one st at each end of next row and fol 3 alt rows. (15 sts.) Place marker at beg of last row.
Work 13 rows st st without shaping, beg with p row.
Shape face
Next row: K2tog, k to end.
Dec one st at same end of next row and fol 3 alt rows. (10 sts.)
Work 5 rows st st.
Dec one st at each end of next row and fol 2 alt rows. (4 sts.) Cast off.
Work another side to match this one, rev face shaping.

HEAD GUSSET

Work as for body gusset but work only 25 rows st st between shapings.

LEGS (make 4)

Using B, cast on 14 sts and work 20 rows. Cast off.

HOOVES (make 4)

Using B only, cast on 4 sts and k 1 row.
Next row: P, inc 1 st at each end.
Work 3 rows st st.
Next row: K, dec 1 st at each end.
P 1 row.
Cast off.

MANE

Using B, cast on 51 sts and k 1 row.
Next row: * K1, k next st in the usual way but do not slip st off LHN. Insert RHN into back of the same st, wind yarn round first and second fingers at back of work, then complete st, slipping original st off N at same time. Yon, and pass previous st (both loops) over the yon. Rep from * to last st, k1.
Rep last 2 rows once more.
Cast off.

TAIL

Using B, cast on 5 sts and work 10 rows st st.
Cast off.

TO MAKE UP

Stitch body gusset to lower edges of

body from end of cast-on row to end of cast-off row. Stitch rem edges tog, leaving section from marker to beg of cast-off row open for neck. Fill. Stitch head gusset along shaped edge of face from end of cast-on row to end of cast-off row. Stitch rem edges tog, leaving section from marker to end of cast-on row open for neck. Fill and stitch to body. Stitch side edges of legs and stitch hooves to cast-on edges and fill. Stitch to body. Stitch ears tog in pairs and stitch to head. Stitch mane along centre of back of head and body. Stitch side edges of tail and stitch to body. Make a small fringe from B and attach to end of tail. Cut eyes from black and white felt and stitch to face.

KENNY KOALA

MATERIALS
Approx 100 g (4 oz) of light brown and 50g (2 oz) of cream DK; a small ball of the same yarn in dark brown; one pair of 3.75 mm (No. 9) knitting needles; polyester filling; 1 m (1 yd) ribbon.

HEIGHT
Approx 30 cm (12 in).

ABBREVIATIONS
See page 7.

Note: entire koala is worked in gst.

LEGS (make 2)
Using LB, cast on 24 sts and k 1 row.
Next row: Inc in first st, k10, inc in next 2 sts, k10, inc in last st. (28 sts.)
K 1 row.
Next row: Inc in first st, k12, inc in next 2 sts, k12, inc in last st. (32 sts.)
K 28 rows.
Cast off.

ARMS (make 2)
Using LB, cast on 18 sts and k 1 row.
Next row: Inc in first st, k7, inc in next 2 sts, k7, inc in last st. (22 sts.)
K 1 row.
Next row: Inc in first st, k9, inc in next 2 sts, k9, inc in last st. (26 sts.)
K 26 rows.
Cast off.

LOWER BODY (make 2)
Using C, cast on 18 sts and k 1 row.
Cast on 3 sts at beg of next 4 rows. (30 sts.)
K 22 rows.
Cast off 2 sts at beg of next 10 rows. (10 sts.)
Cast off.

UPPER BODY (make 2)
Using LB, cast on 14 sts and k 4 rows.
Next row: K2tog, k to end.
Next 3 rows: K to end.

Rep last 4 rows five times more. (8 sts.)
K 2 rows.
Next row: Inc in first st, k to end.
Next 3 rows: K to end.
Rep last 4 rows five times more. (14 sts.) Cast off.

HEAD (make 2)
Using LB, cast on 16 sts and k 1 row.
Inc 1 st at each end of next 7 rows. (30 sts.)
K 26 rows.
Dec 1 st at each end of next 8 rows. (14 sts.)
Cast off.

NOSE
Using DB, cast on 6 sts and k 1 row.
Next row: Inc 1 st at each end. (8 sts.)
K 10 rows.
Dec 1 st at each end of next row. (6 sts.)
Cast off.

EARS (make 4)
Using C, cast on 16 sts and k 14 rows.

Dec 1 st at each end of next 4 rows. (8 sts.)
Cast off.

CLAWS (make 4)
Using DB, cast on 8 sts and k 1 row.
Next row: Cast off 4 sts, k to end.
Next row: K4, cast on 4 sts.
Next 2 rows: K to end.
Rep last 4 rows three times more.
Cast off.

TO MAKE UP
Fold legs and arms in half and stitch side seams. Stitch claws to cast-on edges and fill. Stitch shaped side of upper body sections to cast-off edge of lower body sections and stitch side seams, leaving approx 4 cm (1½ in) open at top for filling. Fill. Stitch head sections tog, leaving cast-on edges open for filling. Fill and stitch to body. Stitch arms and legs to body. Stitch ears tog in pairs and brush with a wire brush to fluff; stitch to head. Stitch nose to head, filling lightly. Embroider features. Tie ribbon around neck.

ERICA ELEPHANT

MATERIALS
Approx 100 g (4 oz) of DK in pink
and a length of the same yarn in
black for eyes; one pair 3.75 mm
(No. 9) knitting needles; large
safety pin; polyester filling.

HEIGHT
Approx 25 cm (10 in).

ABBREVIATIONS
See page 7.

Note: entire elephant is worked
in pink.

BODY AND LEGS
Begin at front leg
* Cast on 16 sts and work 16 rows
st st.*
Break off yarn and leave sts on spare
N. Work from * to *.
Next row: K across last 16 sts, cast
on 8, k across sts on spare N.
(40 sts.) **
Work 21 rows st st.
Shape back and neck
Next row: Cast off 4 sts, k to last
2 sts, k2tog.
Next row: P2tog, p to end.
Rep last 2 rows five times more.
(4 sts.)
Cast off.
Work other side to match this side,
rev shapings for back and neck.

UNDERBODY (make 2)
Work as for body and legs to **.
Work 7 rows st st.
Cast off.

HEAD
Begin with trunk
Cast on 6 sts. Work 6 rows st st inc
1 st at each end of each row.
(18 sts.)
Next row: K6, cast off 3, k to end.
Work on last 9 sts only, leaving first
6 on safety pin.
Work 15 rows st st. Break off yarn
and leave sts on spare N.

Shape neck
Cast on 14 sts and work
2 rows st st.
Cont in st st, inc 1 st at each end of
next row and fol 3 alt rows. (22 sts.)
P 1 row.
Next row: K to end, cast on 3 sts
and k across 9 sts on spare N.
(34 sts.)
Next row: P2tog, p to end.
Next row: K to end.
Rep last 2 rows seven times more.
Place markers at each end of the last
row. (26 sts.)
Dec 1 st at each end of next 7 rows.
(12 sts.) Cast off.
Work other side of head to match
first side, rev all shapings for trunk
and front head.
Shape trunk tips
Work 3 rows st st across sts from
each safety pin. Cast off.

HEAD GUSSET
Cast on 2 sts and work 2 rows st st.
Next row: Inc in both sts.
P 1 row.
Inc 1 st at each end of next row and
fol 2 alt rows. (10 sts.)
Work 12 rows st st.
Dec 1 st at each end of next row and
fol 3 alt rows. (2 sts.)
P 1 row. Cast off.

EARS (make 2)
Cast on 20 sts and k 1 row.
Cont in gst, inc 1 st at each end of

next row and fol 5 alt rows. (32 sts.)
K 14 rows.
Dec 1 st at each end of next 3 rows.
(26 sts.)
Cast off.

SOLES (make 4)
Cast on 6 sts and work 2 rows st st.
Cont in st st and inc 1 st at each end
of next row and fol alt row. (10 sts.)
Work 5 rows st st.
Dec 1 st at each end of next row and
fol alt row. (6 sts.)
P 1 row.
Cast off.

TAIL
Cast on 6 sts and work 16 rows st st.
Next row: (K2tog) 3 times.
Thread yarn through rem sts and
fasten off.

TO MAKE UP
Stitch cast-off edges of two
underbody pieces tog. Stitch body
legs to underbody legs leaving cast-
on edges open. Stitch soles to cast-
on edges. Stitch rem sides of body
tog, leaving neck open for filling. Fill
firmly. Stitch head gusset to head
pieces between markers. Stitch rem
head and trunk seams leaving cast-
on edges open for neck. Fill firmly
(especially trunk) and stitch to body.
Make a pleat in centre of cast-off
edge of each ear and stitch to head.
Stitch side seam of tail and stitch to
body. Embroider eyes.

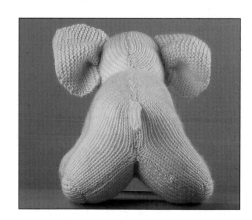

MANDY MONKEY

MATERIALS
Approx 100 g (4 oz) of DK in grey, 25 g (1 oz) of the same yarn in charcoal, and small balls of cream and yellow for the banana; one pair 3.75 mm (No. 9) knitting needles; polyester filling; small pieces of felt in black and white for features.

HEIGHT
Approx 43 cm (17 in).

ABBREVIATIONS
See page 7.

Note: entire monkey is worked in gst.

BODY (make 2)
Using G, cast on 18 sts and k 1 row.
Cast on 3 sts at beg of next 4 rows.
(30 sts.)
K 44 rows.
Cast off 4 sts at beg of next 4 rows.
(14 sts.)
Cast off.

HEAD (make 2)
Using G, cast on 14 sts and k 1 row.
Inc 1 st at each end of next row and fol 2 alt rows. (20 sts.)
Place marker at each end of last row.
K 22 rows.
Dec 1 st at each end of next row and fol 3 alt rows. (12 sts.)
K 1 row.
Cast off.

LOWER JAW
Using G, cast on 15 sts.
Next row: (K3, inc in next st) 3 times, k 3. (18 sts.)
Inc 1 st at each end of next row and fol 3 alt rows. (26 sts.)
K 3 rows.
Cast off.

EARS (make 4)
Using CH, cast on 8 sts and k 8 rows.
Dec 1 st at each end of next 2 rows. (4 sts.) Cast off.

ARMS (make 2)
Using CH, cast on 10 sts.
Next row: Inc in first st, k3, inc in next 2 sts, k3, inc in last st.
(14 sts.)
K 5 rows.
Next row: K6, inc in next 2 sts, k6.
Next row: K7, inc in next 2 sts, k7.
(18 sts.)
K 4 rows.
Change to G.
Next row: K5, inc in next st, k6, inc in next st, k5.
(20 sts.)
K 29 rows.
Dec 1 st at each end of next row and fol 5 alt rows.
(8 sts.)
Cast off.

LEGS (make 2)
Using CH, cast on 10 sts.
Next row: Inc in each st.
(20 sts.)
K 8 rows.
Change to G and k 42 rows.

Dec 1 st at each end of next row and fol 4 alt rows. (10 sts.)
Cast off.

TAIL
Using CH, cast on 4 sts.
Next row: Inc in each st.
K 1 row.
Next row: Inc in each st. (16 sts.)
K 80 rows.
Cast off.

BANANA
Using C, cast on 5 sts and k 1 row.
Next row: Inc in each st. (10 sts.)
K 18 rows.
Next row: (K2tog) 5 times. (5 sts.)
K 1 row.
Thread yarn through rem sts, draw up, and secure.

BANANA SKIN (make 3)
Using Y, cast on 3 sts and k 1 row.
Next row: Inc 1 st at each end.
(5 sts).
K 20 rows.
Dec 1 st at each end of next row.
K 1 row.
K3tog; fasten off.

TO MAKE UP
Stitch side edges of body tog, leaving cast-off edges open for neck. Fill. Stitch cast-off edge of lower jaw to one piece of head between markers. Stitch completed face to remaining head piece leaving cast-on edges open for neck. Fill and stitch to body. Stitch cast-on and side edges of arms and legs to beg of top shaping. Fill and stitch to body. Stitch cast-on and side edges of tail, fill lightly and stitch to lower body. Stitch ears tog in pairs and stitch to sides of head. Stitch side seam of banana and fill. Stitch sides of skins tog, for approx half the length. Secure skin to banana and secure banana to monkey's hand. Cut eyes and nostrils from black and white felt and stitch in place. Using CH, embroider a mouth along seam.

DOLORES DUCK
AND DEBBIE DUCKLING

MATERIALS
Approx 100 g (4 oz) of DK in
yellow and small balls of same
yarn in red and dark brown; one
pair of 3.75 mm (No. 9) knitting
needles; polyester filling;
crochet hook.

HEIGHT
Mrs Dolores Duck: approx 20 cm
(8 in).
Debbie Duckling: approx 13 cm (5 in).

ABBREVIATIONS
See page 7.

Note: ducks (excluding hats) worked
entirely in gst.

MRS DOLORES DUCK

BODY AND HEAD (make 2)
Using Y, cast on 16 sts and k 1 row.
Inc 1 st at each end of next row and
fol 10 alt rows. (38 sts.) Place
markers at each end of last row.
K 3 rows.
Next row: Inc 1 st at each end.
(40 sts.)
K 5 rows.
Next row: K14, cast off 8, k to end.
Work on these last 18 sts only
for tail.
Shape tail
Next row: Inc in first st, k to end.
Next row: Cast off 4, k to end.
Next row: K to end.
Next row: Cast off 4, k to end.
Rep last 4 rows once more. (4 sts.)
K 1 row.
Cast off.
Shape head
Rejoin yarn to rem 14 sts and work
head as follows:
Dec 1 st at each end of next row and
fol 2 alt rows. (8 sts.)
K 1 row.

Inc 1 st at each end of next row and
fol 4 alt rows. (18 sts.)
K 10 rows. Place markers at each
end of last row.
Dec 1 st at each end of next row and
fol 4 alt rows. (8 sts.)
Cast off.

HEAD GUSSET
Using Y, cast on 2 sts and k 2 rows.
Next row: Inc in both sts.
K 2 rows.
Inc 1 st at each end of next row.
(6 sts.)
K 24 rows.
Dec 1 st at each end of next row and
fol fourth row. (2 sts.)
K 2 rows.
Cast off.

BASE GUSSET
Using Y, cast on 2 sts and k 1 row.
Next row: Inc in both sts.
Next 2 rows: K to end.
Next row: Inc 1 st at each end.
Rep last 3 rows twice more. (10 sts.)
K 26 rows.
Next row: Dec 1 st at each end.
Next 2 rows: K to end.
Rep last 3 rows three times more.
(2 sts.)
Cast off.

WINGS (make 4)
Using Y, cast on 8 sts and k 1 row.
Inc 1 st at each end of next row and
fol 3 alt rows. (16 sts.)
K 16 rows.
Dec 1 st at each end of next row and
fol 3 alt rows. (8 sts.)
Cast off.

BEAK (make 2)
Using DB, cast on 2 sts and k 1 row.
Next row: Inc in both sts.
K 1 row.
Inc 1 st at each end of next row.
(6 sts.)
K 6 rows.
Cast off.

FEET (made in one piece)
Using DB, cast on 10 sts and
k 1 row.
Next row: Cast off 4 sts, k to end.
Next row: K6, cast on 4 sts.
Next 2 rows: K to end.
Rep last 4 rows six times more.
(10 sts.)
Cast off.

BONNET
Using R, cast on 40 sts and k 5 rows.
Next row: K3, p34, k3.
Next row: K to end.
Rep last 2 rows eight times more.
Cast off.

TO MAKE UP
Stitch base gusset along cast-on
edge of body and up to marker at
front edge on both body sections.
Stitch head gusset to both sections
between markers. Stitch rem edges
tog, leaving approx 6 cm (2½ in)
open on back of body for filling. Fill
firmly and close opening. Stitch
wings tog in pairs and stitch firmly to
sides of body. Stitch cast-off edges
of beak tog (fold duckling's beak in
half) and stitch to face. For duck,
stitch back seam of bonnet and
crochet chains from cast-on corners
to form ties. Embroider eyes in DB.
Stitch feet to body base. Crochet a
22-cm (9-in) chain using R, tie into a
bow, and stitch to duckling's head.

DEBBIE DUCKLING

BODY AND HEAD (make 2)
Using Y, cast on 8 sts and k 1 row.
Inc 1 st at each end of next 6 alt
rows. (20 sts.) Place markers at each
end of last row.
K 1 row.
Next row: Inc in first st, k to end.
Next row: K to end.
Rep last 2 rows three times more.
(24 sts.)

Next row: Inc in first st, k8, cast off 8, k to end.
Work on these last 7 stitches only for head.

Shape head
Inc 1 st at each end of next row and fol 2 alt rows. (13 sts.)
K 8 rows. Place markers at each end of last row.
Dec 1 st at each end of next row and fol 3 alt rows. (5 sts.) Cast off.

Shape tail
Rejoin yarn to inside edge of rem 10 sts and complete tail as follows:
Next row: Cast off 2 sts, k to end.
Next row: K to last 2 sts, k2tog.
Rep last 2 rows once more.
(4 sts.) Cast off.

BODY GUSSET
* Using Y, cast on 2 sts and k 2 rows.

Next row: Inc in both sts. *
Next 2 rows: K to end.
Next row: Inc 1 st at each end.
Rep last 3 rows once more.
(8 sts.)
K 24 rows.
Next row: Dec 1 st at each end.
Next 2 rows: K to end.
Rep last 3 rows twice more.
(2 sts.)
Next row: K to end.
Next row: K2tog; fasten off.

HEAD GUSSET
Work as for body gusset from * to *.
Next row: Inc 1 st at each end.
(6 sts.)
K 12 rows.
Dec 1 st at each end of next row and fol alt row.
(2 sts.)

K 1 row.
Next row: K2tog; fasten off.

WINGS (make 2)
Using Y, cast on 10 sts and k 16 rows.
Dec 1 st at each end of next 4 rows.
(2 sts.)
Next row: K2tog; fasten off.

BEAK (make 2)
Using DB, cast on 3 sts and k 10 rows.
Cast off.

FEET
Work as for Dolores Duck (page 24).

TO MAKE UP
Work as for Dolores Duck (page 24), stitching single wings to body.

PRISCILLA PIG

MATERIALS
Approx 80 g (3$\frac{1}{2}$ oz) of DK in pink and a small ball of same yarn in black for features and collar; one pair 3.75 mm (No. 9) knitting needles; polyester filling; small piece of black felt.

LENGTH
Approx 22 cm (9 in).

ABBREVIATIONS
See page 7.

Note: entire pig, except hooves, ears and collar, is worked in st st.

BODY
Using PK, cast on 8 sts.
Next row: Inc in each st. (16 sts.)
P 1 row.
Next row: * K2, m1, rep from * to last 2 sts, k2.
P 1 row.
Next row: * K3, m1, rep from * to last 2 sts, k2. (30 sts.)
P 1 row.
Next row: * K4, m1, rep from * to last 2 sts, k2.
P 1 row.
Next row: * K5, m1, rep from * to last 2 sts, k2. (44 sts.)
Work 31 rows st st, beg with p row.
Next row: * K4, k2tog, rep from * to last 2 sts, k2.
P 1 row.
Next row: * K3, k2tog, rep from * to last 2 sts, k2. (30 sts.)
P 1 row.
Next row: * K2, k2tog, rep from * to last 2 sts, k2.
P 1 row.
Next row: * K1, k2tog, rep from * to last 2 sts, k2. (16 sts.)
P 1 row.
Cast off.

LEGS (make 4)
Using PK, cast on 14 sts and work 14 rows st st.
Cast off.

HOOVES (make 4)
Using PK, cast on 5 sts and k 1 row.
Next row: K, inc 1 st at each end.
K 5 rows.
Next row: K, dec 1 st at each end.
K 1 row. Cast off.

HEAD (make 2)
Using PK, cast on 12 sts and work 2 rows st st.
Cont in st st, inc 1 st at each end of next row and fol 3 alt rows. (20 sts.)
Work 6 rows st st. Place markers at each end of last row.
Dec 1 st at each end of next row and fol 3 alt rows. (12 sts.) Cast off.

HEAD GUSSET
Using PK, cast on 2 sts and work 2 rows st st.
Next row: Inc in both sts.
Cont in st st, inc 1 st at each end of next 3 RS rows. (12 sts.)
Work 12 rows st st.
Dec 1 st at each end of next row and fol 4 RS rows. (2 sts.) Cast off.

EARS (make 2)
Using PK, cast on 8 sts and k 16 rows.
Cont in gst, dec 1 st at each end of next row and fol 2 alt rows. (2 sts.)
Next row: K2tog; fasten off.

TAIL
Using PK, cast on 5 sts and work 30 rows st st.
Cast off.

SNOUT
Using PK, cast on 16 sts and work 6 rows st st.
Next row: (K2tog) 8 times.
Cast off p-wise.

COLLAR
Using B, cast on 4 sts and k 42 rows.
Cast off.

TO MAKE UP
Stitch side seam of body, leaving a short section open for filling; fill. Stitch side seams of legs; stitch hooves to cast-on edges. Fill and stitch to sides of body. Stitch head gusset between markers on head sections. Stitch rem seams, leaving cast-on edges open for filling. Fill and stitch to body. Stitch side and cast-off edges of snout. Fill and stitch to face. Stitch ears to head. Stitch side seam of tail; draw thread up tightly to make tail curl. Stitch to body. Make eyes and nostrils from black felt and secure. Embroider eyelashes. Stitch collar around neck.

LAURA LAMB

MATERIALS
Approx 100 g (4 oz) of a triple knit bouclé-type yarn in cream; a small ball of DK in black; one pair each 3.75 mm (No. 9) and 4 mm (No. 8) knitting needles; polyester filling.

LENGTH
Approx 28 cm (11 in).

ABBREVIATIONS
See page 7.

Note: entire lamb is worked in gst.

BODY (make 2)
Using 4 mm (No. 8) Ns and C, cast on 12 sts and k 1 row.
Inc 1 st at each end of next row and fol 4 alt rows. (22 sts.)
K 34 rows.
Shape neck
Next row: Cast off 2 sts, k to end.
Next row: K2tog, k to end.
Rep last 2 rows three times more. (10 sts.)
Cast off.

HEAD (make 2)
Using 4 mm (No. 8) Ns and C, cast on 10 sts and k 1 row.
Inc 1 st at each end of next row and fol 3 alt rows. (18 sts.) Place markers at each end of last row.
K 9 rows.
Dec 1 st at each end of next row and fol 4 alt rows.
(8 sts.)
Next row: K to end.
Cast off.

HEAD GUSSET
Using 4 mm (No. 8) Ns and C, cast on 3 sts and k 1 row.
Inc 1 st at each end of next row and fol 2 alt rows. (9 sts.)
K 30 rows.
Dec 1 st at each end of next row and fol 2 alt rows. (3 sts.)
K 1 row.
Cast off.

EARS (make 2)
Using 4 mm (No. 8) Ns and C, cast on 9 sts and k 16 rows.
Dec 1 st at each end of next row and fol 2 alt rows. (3 sts.)
K 1 row.
Cast off.

TAIL
Using 4 mm (No. 8) Ns and C, cast on 6 sts and k 10 rows.
Cast off.

NOSE
Using 3.75 mm (No. 9) Ns and B, cast on 16 sts and k 6 rows.
Next row: * K1, k2tog, rep from * to last st, k1.
K 1 row.
Next row: (K2tog) 5 times, k1.
(6 sts.)
Thread yarn through sts, draw up, and secure.

HOOVES
Using 3.75 mm (No. 9) Ns and B, cast on 5 sts and k 1 row.
Next row: Inc 1 st at each end.
K 6 rows.
Dec 1 st at each end of next row.
(5 sts.)
K 1 row.
Cast off.

TO MAKE UP
Stitch body sections tog, leaving neck open for filling. Fill. Stitch head gusset to head sections between markers, leaving cast-on edges open for neck. Fill and stitch to body. Stitch side seams of legs and stitch hooves to cast-on edges. Fill and stitch to body. Stitch side and cast-on edges of tail and stitch to body. Stitch ears to head. Stitch side seam of nose, fill, and stitch to head. Embroider eyes using B.

BETSY BEE

MATERIALS
Approx 50 g (2 oz) each of DK in black and yellow; one pair of 3.75 mm (No. 9) knitting needles; polyester filling; small pieces of felt in black and yellow for eyes.

LENGTH
Approx 18 cm (7 in).

ABBREVIATIONS
See page 7.

Note: bee is knitted in st st, except for legs and wings.

BODY
Using B, cast on 8 sts.
Next row: Inc in each st. (16 sts.)
Work 3 rows st st, beg with p row.
Next row: * K1, inc in next st, rep from * to end.
Work 3 rows st st, beg with p row.
Next row: * K2, inc in next st, rep from * to end. (32 sts.)
Work 3 rows st st, beg with p row.
Next row: * K3, inc in next st, rep from * to end.
Work 3 rows st st, beg with p row.
Next row: * K4, inc in next st, rep from * to end. (48 sts.)
P 1 row. Cont in stripe patt:
Work 2 rows st st using Y.
Work 2 rows st st using B.
Rep these 4 rows four times more.
Work 2 rows st st using Y.
Cont in B only:
Next row: * K4, k2tog, rep from * to end.
Work 3 rows st st, beg with p row.
Next row: * K3, k2tog, rep from * to end. (32 sts.)
Work 3 rows st st, beg with p row.
Next row: * K2, k2tog, rep from * to end. (24 sts.)
P 1 row.
Next row: * K1, k2tog, rep from * to end. (16 sts.)
P 1 row.
Next row: (K2tog) 8 times.
P 1 row.

Thread yarn through sts, draw up, and fasten off.

LEGS (make 6)
Using B, cast on 5 sts and k 20 rows. Cast off.

WINGS (make 2)
Using B, cast on 12 sts; k 20 rows.

Dec 1 st at each end of next 3 rows. (6 sts.) Cast off.

TO MAKE UP
Stitch side seam of body, leaving 5 cm (2 in) open for filling. Fill. Stitch side seams of legs; stitch to underside of body. Stitch wings to top. Cut eyes from felt; stitch to face.

CORA CATERPILLAR

MATERIALS
Approx 50 g (2 oz) of green, lilac and black DK; one pair 3.75 mm (No. 9) knitting needles; polyester filling; small pieces of felt in black and white for eyes.

LENGTH
Approx 58 cm (23 in).

ABBREVIATIONS
See page 7.

BODY
Using GR, cast on 8 sts.
Next row: Inc in each st. (16 sts.)
Work 3 rows st st, beg with p row.
Next row: * K1, inc in next st, rep from * to end.
Work 3 rows st st, beg with p row.
Next row: * K2, inc in next st, rep from * to end. (32 sts.)
Work 3 rows st st, beg with p row.
Next row: * K3, inc in next st, rep from * to end.
(40 sts.)
Work 18 rows st st, beg with p row.
**** Next row:** * P2tog, rep from * to end. (20 sts.)
Change to B and k 4 rows.
Next row: Change to L, and k, inc in each st. (40 sts.) Work 18 rows st st, beg with p row ** . Rep from ** to ** four times more, alternating GR and L yarn for each segment.
Next row: * P2tog, rep from * to end. (20 sts.)
Change to B and k 4 rows.
Change to GR and work tail as follows:
Work 8 rows st st.
Cont in st st and dec 1 st at each end of every RS row until 4 sts rem.
Thread yarn through sts; fasten off.

RIGHT LEGS (make 10)
Using B, cast on 12 sts and work 4 rows st st.
Next row: Cast off 7 sts, k to end. (5 sts.)
Work 9 rows st st, beg with p row. Cast off.

LEFT LEGS (make 10)
Using B, cast on 5 sts and work 10 rows st st.
Next row: Cast on 7 sts, k to end. (12 sts.)
Work 4 rows st st, beg with p row. Cast off.

FEELERS (make 2)
Using B, cast on 5 sts and work 24 rows st st. Thread yarn through sts, draw up, and secure.

TO MAKE UP
Stitch side edges of body from head to tail, leaving about 5 cm (2 in) open in middle for filling. Fill. Stitch legs tog in pairs, fill and stitch a pair on each side of body segments. Stitch side seams of feelers and pull thread tight to make feelers curl. Secure and stitch to head. Cut eyes from black and white felt and stitch to face. Embroider mouth using B.

FREDDIE FROG

MATERIALS

Approx 50 g (2 oz) of DK in green and 25 g (1 oz) of the same yarn in yellow; one pair 3.75 mm (No. 9) knitting needles; polyester filling; small pieces of felt in black and red for features.

LENGTH

Approx 20 cm (8 in).

ABBREVIATIONS

See page 7.

Note: entire frog is worked in gst.

BODY (make 2)

Using GR, cast on 3 sts and k 1 row.
Inc 1 st at each end of next row and fol 9 alt rows. (23 sts.)
K 28 rows.
Cast off 4 sts at beg of next 4 rows. (7 sts.) Cast off.

GUSSET (make 2)

Using GR, cast on 2 sts and k 2 rows.
Next row: Inc in both sts.
(4 sts.)
K 4 rows.
Inc 1 st at each end of next row and every fifth row until 10 sts on N.
K 50 rows.
Cast off.

BACK LEGS (make 4)

Using Y, cast on 20 sts and
k 6 rows.
Next row: Cast off 10 sts, k to end.
(10 sts.)
K 11 rows.
Next row: K2tog, k to end.
Next row: K to end.
Rep last 2 rows twice more.
(7 sts.)
Cast off.

FRONT LEGS (make 4)

Using Y, cast on 9 sts and k 4 rows.
Next row: Cast off 5 sts, k to end.
(4 sts.)

K 6 rows.
Cast off.

FEET (make 4)

Using Y, cast on 6 sts and k 1 row.
***Next row:** Cast off 3 sts, k to end.
Next row: K 3, cast on 3 sts.
K 2 rows. *
Rep from * to * once more.
Cast off.

EYES (make 2)

Using GR, cast on 5 sts and k 1 row.
Inc 1 st at each end of next row.
(7 sts.)
K 4 rows.
Dec 1 st at each end of next row.
(5 sts.)

K 1 row.
Cast off.

TO MAKE UP

Stitch cast-off edges of gusset pieces tog. Stitch gusset to sides of body, placing tapered ends at cast-on edge of body, leaving approx 5 cm (2 in) open for filling. Fill and close. Stitch back legs tog in pairs, fill, and stitch to back and sides of body. Stitch front legs tog in pairs, fill, and stitch to body. Stitch a foot to the end of each leg. Run a gathering thread round edges of eyes, draw up to form a ball, fill, and stitch to top of head. Cut eyes and mouth from felt and stitch to face.

TIMOTHY TORTOISE

MATERIALS
Approx 50 g (2 oz) each of yellow and green DK; a small ball of the same yarn in red; one pair of 3.75 mm (No. 9) knitting needles; polyester filling; small pieces of felt in black and red for features.

LENGTH
Approx 30 cm (12 in).

ABBREVIATIONS
See page 7.

Note: entire tortoise is worked in gst.

SHELL SEGMENTS
(make 5 Y and 1 GR)
Cast on 3 sts and k 1 row.
Inc 1 st at each end of next row and fol 4 alt rows.* (13 sts.)
Next 3 rows: K to end.
Next row: K1, k2tog, k to last 3 sts, k2tog, k1.
Rep last 4 rows twice more. (7 sts.)
K 1 row.
Cast off.

SHELL SEGMENTS FOR EDGE
(make 5 GR)
Work as for whole segments to *.
K 1 row.
Inc 1 st at each end of next row and fol alt row. (17 sts.)
K 2 rows.
Cast off.

BASE
Using Y, cast on 10 sts and k 1 row.
Inc 1 st at each end of next row and fol 7 alt rows. (26 sts.)
K 32 rows.
Dec 1 st at each end of next row and fol 7 alt rows. (10 sts.)
K 1 row.
Cast off.

LEGS (make 4)
Using Y, cast on 20 sts and k 18 rows.
Cast off.

HEAD
Using Y, cast on 16 sts and k 1 row.
Next row: Inc in first st, k6, inc in next 2 sts, k6, inc in last st.
K 1 row.
Next row: Inc in first st, k8, inc in next 2 sts, k8, inc in last st.
(24 sts.)
K 8 rows.
Next row: * K2, k2tog, rep from * to end.
(18 sts.)
K 6 rows.
Cast off.

TAIL
Using Y, cast on 8 sts and k 10 rows.
Next row: (K2tog) 4 times.
Thread yarn through rem sts, draw up, and secure.

HAT
CROWN
Using R, cast on 14 sts and k 8 rows.
Next row: (K2tog) 7 times.
Thread yarn through rem sts, draw up, fasten off, and stitch side seam.

BRIM
Using R, cast on 5 sts and k 44 rows. Cast off and stitch cast-on and cast-off edges tog. Gather side edge of brim and stitch to crown.

TO MAKE UP
Stitch shell sections tog as per diagram. Stitch top to base, leaving 5 cm (2 in) of seam open for filling. Fill. Stitch side and cast-on edges of legs, head and tail. Fill and stitch to shell. Cut eyes and mouth from felt and stitch to face. Stitch hat to head.

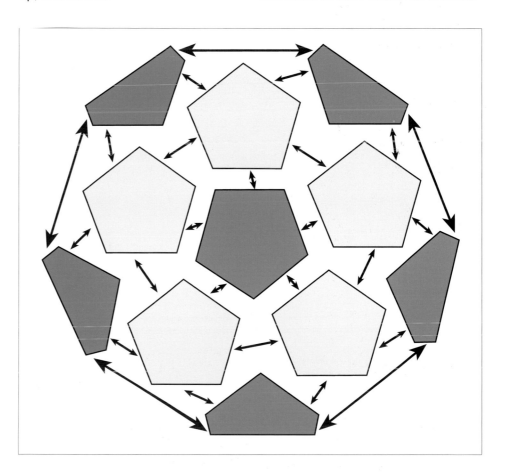

SERENA SNAIL

LENGTH
Approx 22 cm (9 in).

ABBREVIATIONS
See page 7.

SHELL
Using L, cast on 8 sts.
Next row: K, inc in each st. (16 sts.)
P 1 row.
Next row: * K1, inc in next st, rep from * to end. (24 sts.)
P 1 row.
Next row: * K2, inc in next st, rep from * to end. (32 sts.)
Work 4 rows st st, beg with p row.
Next row: * P2, p2tog, rep from * to end. (24 sts.)
Change to B and k 4 rows.
Next row: Change to M and inc k-wise in each st. (48 sts.)
Work 8 rows st st, beg with p row.
Next row: * P2, p2tog, rep from * to end. (36 sts.)
Change to B and k 4 rows.
Next row: Change to L and inc k-wise in each st. (72 sts.)
Work 8 rows st st, beg with p row.
Next row: * P2, p2tog, rep from * to end.
Change to B and k 4 rows. (54 sts.)
Cast off.

BASE
Using M, cast on 10 sts and work 2 rows st st.
Cont in st st and inc 1 st at each end of next row and fol 4 alt rows. (20 sts.)
Work 7 rows st st, beg with p row.
Dec 1 st at each end of next row and fol 4 alt rows. (10 sts.)
P 1 row. Cast off.

BODY
Using M, cast on 6 sts.
Next row: K, inc in each st. (12 sts.)
P 1 row.
Next row: * K1, inc in next st, rep from * to end. (18 sts.)
P 1 row.
Next row: * K2, inc in next st, rep from * to end. (24 sts.)
P 1 row.
Next row: * K3, inc in next st, rep from * to end. (30 sts.)
Work 39 rows st st, beg with p row.
Next row: * K3, k2tog, rep from * to end. (24 sts.)
P 1 row.
Next row: * K2, k2tog, rep from * to end. (18 sts.)
P 1 row.
Next row: * K1, k2tog, rep from * to end. (12 sts.)
P 1 row.

Next row: (K2tog) 6 times. (6 sts.)
P 1 row.
Next row: (K2tog) 3 times.
Thread yarn through sts, draw up, and secure.

FEELERS
Using B, cast on 4 sts and k 16 rows.
Thread yarn through sts, draw up, and secure.

TO MAKE UP
Stitch side seam of shell and stitch base to cast-off edge, leaving approx 5 cm (2 in) open for filling. Fill and close. Stitch side edge of body, leaving 5 cm (2 in) open for filling. Fill and close and stitch top of body to base of shell as in photograph. Stitch sides of feelers, draw up tightly so that they curl up, and stitch to face. Stitch eyes to face.

SYDNEY SNAKE

MATERIALS
Approx 25 g (1 oz) each of DK in black, yellow and green; one pair 3.75 mm (No. 9) knitting needles; polyester filling; small pieces of felt in black, white and red for features.

LENGTH
Approx 90 cm (36 in).

ABBREVIATIONS
See page 7.

BODY
Begin at head
Using B, cast on 7 sts.

Next row: K, inc in each st. (14 sts.)
P 1 row.
Next row: * K1, inc in next st, rep from * to end. (21 sts.)
P 1 row.
Next row: * K2, inc in next st, rep from * to end. (28 sts.)
P 1 row.
Next row: * K3, inc in next st, rep from * to end. (35 sts.)
Work 19 rows st st beg with p row.
Change to Y and work 6 rows st st.
Change to GR and work 6 rows st st.
Change to B and work 6 rows st st.
Rep last 18 rows nine times more.
Change to Y and work 6 rows st st.
Change to B:
Next row: * K 3, k2tog, rep from *

to end. Work 7 rows st st, beg with p row.
Next row: * K2, k2tog, rep from * to end.
(21 sts.)
Work 7 rows st st, beg with p row.
Next row: * K 1, k2tog, rep from * to end.
Work 7 rows st st, beg with p row.
Next row: (K2tog) 7 times.
Thread yarn through rem 7 sts, draw up, and secure.

TO MAKE UP
Stitch side seam, leaving approx 5 cm (2 in) open for filling. Fill and close. Cut eyes and tongue from felt and stitch to face.

CLAUDE CROCODILE

MATERIALS
50 g (2 oz) green and a small ball of the same yarn in red; one pair 3.75 mm (No. 9) knitting needles; polyester filling; small pieces of felt in black and white for eyes.

LENGTH
Approx 45 cm (18 in).

ABBREVIATIONS
See page 7.

Note: entire crocodile is worked in gst.

BODY (make 2)
Begin at head
* Using GR, cast on 3 sts and k 2 rows.
Inc 1 st at each end of next row and every fol third row until 21 sts on N.*
K 18 rows.
Dec 1 st at each end of next row and every fol third row until 13 sts rem.
K 2 rows.
Inc 1 st at each end of next row and fol 4 alt rows.
K 4 rows, inc 1 st at each end of fourth row.
(25 sts.)
K 36 rows.
Dec 1 st at each end of next row and every fol third row until 11 sts rem.
K 24 rows.
Dec 1 st at each end of next row and fol 3 alt rows. (3 sts.)
Cast off.

MOUTH (make 2)
Using R, work as for body from * to *.
Cast off.

FEET (make 8)
Using GR, cast on 11 sts and k 6 rows.
Next row: Cast off 5 sts, k to end. (6 sts.)
K 6 rows.
Cast off.

SPINE (make 2)
Using GR, cast on 2 sts and * k 1 row.
Inc 1 st at beg of next row and fol 2 alt rows. (5 sts.)
K 1 row, thus ending at curved edge.
Dec 1 st at beg of next row and fol 2 alt rows. (2 sts.) *
Rep from * to * 11 times more.
Cast off.

TO MAKE UP
Stitch cast-off edges of mouth together and stitch mouth to relevant edges of head. Stitch lower mouth to body across cast-off edge of mouth, thus preventing the filling from entering the lower mouth. Stitch rem edges of body, leaving approx 5 cm (2 in) open for filling. Fill and close. Stitch feet tog in pairs, fill, and stitch to sides of body.

Stitch spines along top of body, beg at neck and end just before end of tail. Cut eyes from black and white felt and stitch to face.

DELIA DINOSAUR

MATERIALS
Approx 50 g (2 oz) of DK in lilac and a small ball of the same yarn in blue; one pair 3.75 mm (No. 9) knitting needles; polyester filling; small pieces of felt in black, red and white for features.

HEIGHT
Approx 28 cm (11 in).

ABBREVIATIONS
See page 7.

Note: entire dinosaur is worked in gst.

BODY (make 2)
Using L, cast on 40 sts and k 1 row.
Inc 1 st at each end of next row and fol alt row. (44 sts.)
K 7 rows.
Cast off 3 sts at beg of next row and at same edge on fol 3 alt rows. (32 sts.)
Cast off 2 sts at same edge on next 4 alt rows. (24 sts.)
Dec 1 st at same edge on next 4 alt rows.
Dec 1 st at same edge on every fourth row until 16 sts rem.
K 13 rows.
Dec 1 st at each end of next row and fol 2 alt rows. (10 sts.) Place marker at each end of last row.
K 1 row.
Inc 1 st at each end of next row and fol 2 alt rows. (16 sts.)
K 9 rows. Place markers at each end of last row.
Dec 1 st at each end of next row and fol 4 alt rows. (8 sts.)
Cast off.

BODY GUSSET
Using L, cast on 3 sts and k 2 rows.
Inc 1 st at each end of next row and every fol third row until 13 sts on N.
K 80 rows.
Dec 1 st at each end of next row and every fol third row until 3 sts rem.

K 2 rows.
Cast off.

HEAD GUSSET
Using L, cast on 3 sts and k 2 rows.
Inc 1 st at each end of next row and fol 2 alt rows. (9 sts.)
K 20 rows.
Dec 1 st at each end of next row and fol 2 alt rows. (3 sts.)
K 2 rows.
Cast off.

SPINE
Using BL, cast on 3 sts and
* k 1 row.
Inc 1 st at beg of next row and at same edge on fol 4 alt rows. (8 sts.)
K 1 row, thus ending at shaped edge.
Dec 1 st at beg of next row and at same edge on fol 4 alt rows. (3 sts.) *
Rep from * to * five times more.
K 1 row.
Cast off.

FEET (make 4)
Using BL, cast on 14 sts and k 3 rows.

* **Next row:** Cast off 4 sts, k to end.
Next row: K9, cast on 4 sts.
K 4 rows. *
Rep from * to * once more.
Cast off.

ARMS (make 4)
Using BL, cast on 12 sts and k 7 rows.
Next row: Cast off 6 sts, k to end. (6 sts.)
K 8 rows.
Cast off.

TO MAKE UP
Stitch body gusset to straight sides of body sections from markers at neck to end of cast-on edge. Stitch head gusset to top of head between markers. Stitch rem body edges, stitching spine tog with back edges from neck to tail, leaving approx 5 cm (2 in) open at front neck for filling. Fill and close. Stitch arms tog in pairs, fill, and stitch to body. Stitch feet tog in pairs, fill lightly, and stitch to front of body. Cut eyes and mouth from felt and stitch to face. Embroider BL dots on body along spine.

TOBY TEDDY

MATERIALS

TEDDY
Approx 100 g (4 oz) of DK in beige; a small ball of same yarn in dark brown for nose and features; one pair 3.75 mm (No. 9) knitting needles; polyester filling.

TOGS
Approx 100 g (4 oz), in total, of DK in colours of your choice; one pair each 3.75 mm (No. 9) and 4.5 mm (No. 7) knitting needles.

HEIGHT
Approx 45 cm (18 in).

ABBREVIATIONS
See page 7.

Note: teddy is worked in beige, except for nose, which is worked in dark brown.

TEDDY

LEGS (make 2)
Cast on 29 sts.
Next row: K13, inc in next st, k1, inc in next st, k13.
P 1 row.
Next row: Inc in first st, k13, inc in next st, k1, inc in next st, k13, inc in last st. (35 sts.)
Work 9 rows st st, beg with p row.
Next row: K15, k2tog, k1, k2tog tbl, k15.
Next row: P14, p2tog tbl, p1, p2tog, p14.
Next row: K13, k2tog, k1, k2tog tbl, k13.
Next row: P12, p2tog tbl, p1, p2tog, p12. (27 sts.)
Work 22 rows st st.
Cast off.

ARMS (make 2)
Cast on 18 sts.
Next row: Inc in first st, k7, inc in next 2 sts, k7, inc in last st.
P 1 row.

Next row: Inc in first st, k9, inc in next 2 sts, k9, inc in last st. (26 sts.)
Work 25 rows st st, beg with p row.
Cast off.

BODY (make 2)
Cast on 16 sts and k 1 row.
Cont in st st and cast on 4 sts at beg of next 4 rows. (32 sts.)
Work 39 rows st st, beg with p row.
Cont in st st and cast off 4 sts at beg of next 4 rows. (16 sts.)
Cast off.

HEAD
Cast on 14 sts and work 2 rows st st.
Next row: Inc in first st, k to last st, inc in last st.
Next row: P to end.
Next row: Inc in first st, k to end.
Next row: P to end.
Rep last 4 rows three times more. (26 sts.) Place markers at each end of last row.
Work 4 rows st st.
Next row: K2tog, k to last 2 sts, k2tog.
Next row: P to end.
Next row: K2tog, k to end.
Next row: P to end.
Rep last 4 rows three times more. (14 sts.)
Cast off.
Work another side to match this side, rev shapings.

HEAD GUSSET
Cast on 3 sts and work 2 rows st st.
Inc 1 st at each end of next row and fol 6 alt rows. (17 sts.)
Work 19 rows st st.
Dec 1 st at each end of next row and fol 6 alt rows. (3 sts.)
P 1 row.
Cast off.

SOLES (make 2)
Cast on 5 sts and work 2 rows st st.
Inc 1 st at each end of next row and fol alt row. (9 sts.)
Work 5 rows st st.
Dec 1 st at each end of next row and fol alt row. (5 sts.)

P 1 row.
Cast off.

EARS (make 4)
Cast on 16 sts and work 8 rows st st.
Next row: K1, skpo, k to last 3 sts, k2tog, k1.
Next row: P to end.
Rep last 2 rows once more.
(12 sts.)
Cast off.

NOSE
Using DB, cast on 5 sts and k 6 rows.
Dec 1 st at each end of next row.
K 1 row.
Next row: K3tog; fasten off.

TO MAKE UP
Stitch side seams of legs and stitch soles to cast-on edges. Fill. Stitch cast-on and side edges of arms. Fill. Stitch body sections tog, leaving cast-on edges open. Fill. Stitch gusset to head sections beg and end at markers. Stitch rem seams, leaving cast-on edges open. Stitch head to body and stitch arms and legs in position. Stitch ears tog in pairs and stitch to head. Stitch nose in position, filling lightly. Embroider features.

TOGS
Note: general instructions only are given so that you can make the togs in colours of your choice.

SHORTS
Using 4.5 mm (No. 7) Ns, cast on 64 sts and k 5 rows.
Work 17 rows st st, beg with p row.
Change to 3.75 mm (No. 9) Ns and work 6 rows k1, p1 rib.
Cast off loosely ribwise.

JERSEY
BACK
Using 3.75 mm (No. 9) Ns, cast on 34 sts and work 4 rows k1, p1 rib.
Change to 4.5 mm (No. 7) Ns and work 36 rows st st.
Cast off.

FRONT

Work as for back until 12 rows st st have been completed.

Divide for opening

Next row: K15, cast off 4 sts, k15. Work on these last 15 sts only for first side.

Work 15 rows st st, end with WS row.

Shape neck

Next row: Cast off 4 sts, k to end. Dec 1 st at neck edge on next two RS rows. (9 sts.)

Cont in st st until 36 rows completed, as for back. Rejoin yarn to rem 15 sts and work to match first side, rev shapings.

SLEEVES (make 2)

Using 3.75 mm (No. 9) Ns, cast on 32 sts and work 4 rows k1, p1 rib. Change to 4.5 mm (No. 7) Ns and work 8 rows st st. Cast off.

BANDS (make 2)

Using 3.75 mm (No. 9) Ns, cast on 6 sts and work 18 rows k1, p1 rib. Cast off ribwise.

COLLAR

Using 3.75 mm (No. 9) Ns, cast on 50 sts and work 8 rows k1, p1 rib. Cast off loosely ribwise.

BOOTS AND SOCKS (make 2)

Using 4.5 mm (No. 7) Ns, cast on 31 sts.

Next row: Inc in first st, k13, inc in next st, k1, inc in next st, k13, inc in last st. (35 sts.)

Work 7 rows st st, beg with p row.

Next row: K15, k2tog, k1, k2tog tbl, k15.

Next row: P14, p2tog tbl, p1, p2tog, p14.

Next row: K13, k2tog, k1, k2tog tbl, k13.

Next row: P12, p2tog tbl, p1, p2tog, p12.

Change colour for socks and work 12 rows st st.

K 6 rows. Cast off loosely.

SOLES (make 2)

Using 4.5 mm (No. 7) Ns, cast on 5 sts and work 2 rows st st.

Inc 1 st at each end of next row and fol alt row. (9 sts.)

Work 7 rows st st.

Dec 1 st at each end of next row and fol alt row. (5 sts.)

P 1 row.

Cast off.

TO MAKE UP

SHORTS

Stitch side edges and stitch 3 cm (1¹⁄₂in) of cast-on edge tog at centre to form crotch.

JERSEY

Stitch bands to respective edges of opening. Stitch cast-on edge of collar to neck, beg and end at centre of each band. Stitch side seam for 5 cm (2 in), leaving rem open for armholes. Stitch sleeve seams and stitch sleeves into armholes.

BOOTS

Stitch side seam and stitch sole to cast-on edge. Crochet two chains of approx 25 cm (10 in) and thread through boot shaping for laces.

BRIGHT BALL

MATERIALS
Approx 25 g (1 oz) of DK in each of five bright colours; one pair of 3.75 mm (No. 9) knitting needles; polyester filling.

SIZE
Approx 20 cm (8 in) in diameter.

ABBREVIATIONS
See page 7.

Note: entire ball is worked in gst.

MAIN SECTIONS
(make 8, two in each of 4 colours)
Cast on 3 sts and k 5 rows.
Next row: Inc 1 st at each end.
Next 5 rows: K to end.
Rep last 6 rows four times more.
(13 sts.)
Next row: Dec 1 st at each end.
Next 5 rows: K to end.
Rep last 6 rows five times more.
(3 sts.) Cast off.

BASE SECTIONS
(make 2 using fifth colour)
Cast on 3 sts and k 1 row.

Inc 1 st at each end of next row and fol alt row.
(7 sts.)
K 6 rows.
Dec 1 st at each end of next row and fol alt row.
(3 sts.)
K 1 row. Cast off.

TO MAKE UP
Stitch main sections tog, leaving 5 cm (2 in) of seam open for filling. Fill firmly. Draw ends tog with a gathering thread and stitch base sections to cover.

MORTIMER MUTT

MATERIALS
Approx 100 g (4 oz) DK in white; one pair 3.75 mm (No. 9) knitting needles; polyester filling; small pieces of felt in black and white for features; 1 m (1 yd) ribbon.

LENGTH
Approx 30 cm (12 in).

ABBREVIATIONS
See page 7.

Note: entire dog is worked in gst, and in white, except for features.

OUTER BODY (make 2)
Begin with front leg
* Cast on 13 sts and k 12 rows.
Dec 1 st at beg of next row and at same edge on next 2 rows. (10 sts.)
K 9 rows.*
Break off yarn and leave sts on spare N.
Work back leg
Work as for front leg from * to *, k 1 row, cast on 14 sts and k across sts for front leg. (34 sts.) **
K 28 rows across all sts.
Next row: Cast off 4 sts, k to last 2 sts, k2tog.
Next row: K2 tog, k to end.
Rep last 2 rows until 4 sts rem.
Cast off.

UNDERBODY (make 2)
Work as for body to **.
K 6 rows.
Cast off.

HEAD (make 2)
Cast on 10 sts and k 1 row.
Inc 1 st at each end of next row and fol 3 alt rows.
(18 sts.)
K 20 rows.
Dec 1 st at each end of next row and fol 3 alt rows.
(10 sts.)
K 1 row.
Cast off.

MUZZLE
Cast on 10 sts and k 48 rows.
Cast off.

EARS (make 2)
Cast on 13 sts and k 7 rows.
Dec 1 st at each end of next row and fol 4 alt rows.
K 1 row.
K3tog; fasten off.

SOLES (make 4)
Cast on 3 sts and k 1 row.
Inc 1 st at each end of next 2 rows. (7 sts.)
K 5 rows.
Dec 1 st at each end of next 2 rows. (3 sts.)
K 1 row.
Cast off.

TAIL
Cast on 6 sts and k 18 rows.
Cast off.

TO MAKE UP
Stitch two underbody pieces tog along cast-off edges. Place this underbody between two outer body pieces and stitch leg seams, leaving cast-on edges open for soles. Stitch rem of body tog leaving neck edge open for filling. Stitch soles to cast-on edges of legs. Fill firmly. Fold tail in half, lengthwise, stitch tog, and attach one end to rump of body. Stitch cast-on and cast-off edges of muzzle together. Run a gathering thread along one side, gather, and secure. Fill muzzle. Stitch two head pieces tog, leaving cast-on edges open for neck. Fill. Stitch muzzle in place on lower half of head as in photograph. Stitch ears on securely. Make moustache by cutting 40 lengths of yarn each 14 cm (5½ in) long. Secure in centre and stitch on muzzle. Cut eyes and nose from felt and stitch to face. Stitch head firmly to body. Tie ribbon around neck.

HETTY HOUND

MATERIALS
Approx 100 g (4 oz) DK in beige; a small ball of the same yarn in black; one pair 3.75 mm (No. 9) knitting needles; polyester filling; small pieces of felt in black and white for eyes; 1 m (1 yd) ribbon.

LENGTH
Approx 36 cm (14 in).

ABBREVIATIONS
See page 7.

Note: entire hound is worked in gst. Beige is used throughout, except for nose, which is worked in black.

BODY AND HEAD (make 2)
Cast on 16 sts and k 1 row.
Inc 1 st at each end of next row and fol 6 alt rows. (30 sts.)
K 36 rows.
Shape head
Next row: Inc in first st, k to end.
Next row: K to end.
Rep last 2 rows three times more. (34 sts.)
Next row: Inc in first st, k to end.
Next row: K2tog, k to end.
Rep last 2 rows three times more. Place marker at end of last row.
Next row: K to end.
Next row: K2tog, k to end.
Rep last 2 rows five times more. (28 sts.)
Next row: K2tog, k to end.
Rep last row 5 times more. (22 sts.) Place marker at beg of last row.
Next row: K2tog, k to end.
Next row: K to end.
Rep last 2 rows three times more. (18 sts.)
K 6 rows.
Dec 1 st at each end of next row and fol 3 alt rows. (10 sts.)
Cast off.

BODY GUSSET
Cast on 3 sts and k 2 rows.

Inc 1 st at each end of next row and on every fol third row until 15 sts on N.
K 62 rows.
Dec 1 st at each end of next row and on every fol third row until 3 sts rem.
K 2 rows.
Cast off.

HEAD GUSSET
Cast on 3 sts and k 2 rows.
Inc 1 st at each end of next row and every fol fourth row until 11 sts on N.
K 22 rows.
Dec 1 st at each end of next row and on every fol fourth row until 3 sts rem.
K 2 rows.
Cast off.

EARS (make 2)
Cast on 17 sts and k 1 row.
Inc 1 st at each end of next row and fol alt row. (21 sts.)
K 12 rows.
Dec 1 st at each end of next row and on every fol 12th row until 15 sts rem.
K 20 rows.
Cast off.

FEET (make 2)
Cast on 16 sts.
Next row: Inc in first st, k6, inc in next 2 sts, k6, inc in last st. (20 sts.)
K 1 row.
Next row: Inc in first st, k8, inc in next 2 sts, k8, inc in last st. (24 sts.)
K 24 rows.
Cast off.

TAIL
Cast on 10 sts and k 18 rows.
Dec 1 st at each end of next row and fol 3 alt rows.
Next row: K2tog; fasten off.

NOSE
Using B, cast on 9 sts and k 1 row.
Inc 1 st at each end of next row and fol alt row.
(13 sts.)
K 10 rows.

Dec 1 st at each end of next row and fol alt row. (9 sts.)
K 1 row.
Cast off.

TO MAKE UP
Stitch body gusset to body, beg at top end of cast-on row and end at marker under head. Stitch head gusset to head, beg at lower end of cast-off row and end at marker at back of head. Stitch rem body and head seams, leaving approx 5 cm (2 in) open at back for filling. Fill and stitch closed. Stitch ears to head. Stitch side seam of tail, fill and stitch to body. Stitch side and cast-on edges of feet, fill, and stitch to front of body, as in photograph. Cut eyes from felt and stitch to face. Stitch nose in position, filling lightly. Tie ribbon around neck. Embroider mouth.

PAMELA PUPPY

MATERIALS
Approx 100 g (4 oz) of a triple knit bouclé-type yarn in cream, 50 g (2 oz) of the same yarn in black, and a small ball in pink for collar; one pair 4 mm (No. 8) knitting needles; polyester filling; pieces of felt in black and white for eyes.

LENGTH
Approx 36 cm (14 in).

ABBREVIATIONS
See page 7.

Note: entire dog is worked in gst.

BODY AND LEGS (make 2)
Begin at back leg
* Using C, cast on 12 sts and k 18 rows.
Break off yarn and leave sts on a spare N.
Work front leg and body
Using C, cast on 12 sts and k 18 rows.
Next row: K across sts for front leg, cast on 16 sts, then k across sts for back leg. (40 sts.) *
K 22 rows.
Shape neck
Dec 1 st at beg of next row and at same edge on next 9 rows. (30 sts.)
Cast off.

UNDERBODY (make 2)
Work as for body from * to *.
K 6 rows.
Cast off.

HEAD (make 2)
Using B, cast on 12 sts and k 1 row.
Inc 1 st at each end of next row and fol 4 alt rows. (22 sts.)
Place markers at each end of last row.
K 9 rows.
Dec 1 st at each end of next row and fol 5 alt rows. (10 sts.)
K 1 row.
Cast off.

HEAD GUSSET
Using C, cast on 3 sts and k 1 row.
Inc 1 st at each end of next row and fol 3 alt rows. (11 sts.)
K 36 rows.
Dec 1 st at each end of next row and fol 3 alt rows. (3 sts.)
K 1 row.
Cast off.

EARS (make 2)
Using C, cast on 7 sts and k 1 row.
Inc 1 st at each end of next row and fol 2 alt rows. (13 sts.)
K 26 rows.
Cast off.

SOLES (make 4)
Using B, cast on 5 sts and k 1 row.
Next row: Inc 1 st at each end.
K 6 rows.
Dec 1 st at each end of next row. (5 sts.)
K 1 row.
Cast off.

SPOTS (make 2)
Using B, cast on 7 sts and k 1 row.
Inc 1 st at each end of next row and fol 2 alt rows. (13 sts.)
K 10 rows.
Dec 1 st at each end of next row and

fol 2 alt rows. (7 sts.)
K 1 row. Cast off.

NOSE
Work as for sole.

TAIL
Using B, cast on 7 sts and k 10 rows.
Cast off.

COLLAR
Using PK, cast on 6 sts and k 60 rows. Cast off.

TO MAKE UP
Stitch cast-off edges of two underbody pieces together. Stitch sides of underbody legs to relevant sides of body legs. Stitch soles to cast-on edges of legs. Stitch rem body seams, leaving neck open for filling. Fill. Stitch head gusset to head sections between markers. Stitch rem head seams, leaving cast-on edges open for filling. Fill and stitch to body. Stitch ears to head. Stitch side and cast-on edges of tail; fill and stitch to body. Stitch spots to body. Cut eyes from felt and stitch to face. Stitch nose to face, filling lightly. Stitch cast-on and cast-off edges of collar together.

COCO CAT

MATERIALS

Approx 70 g (3 oz) DK in dark brown and a small ball of the same yarn in beige for features; one pair of 3.75 mm (No. 9) knitting needles; polyester filling; small pieces of felt in black and yellow for eyes; 1 m (1 yd) ribbon.

LENGTH

Approx 23 cm (9 in), excluding tail.

ABBREVIATIONS

See page 7.

Note: entire cat is worked in st st, and in dark brown.

BODY

Cast on 12 sts and work 2 rows st st.
Inc 1 st at each end of next row and fol 3 alt rows. (20 sts.)
Work 33 rows, beg with p row.
Shape neck
Next row: Cast off 2 sts, k to last 2 sts, k2tog.
Next row: P to end.
Rep last 2 rows twice more. (11 sts.)
Cast off.
Work another side to match this one, rev neck shapings.

BODY GUSSET

Cast on 3 sts and work 2 rows.
Inc 1 st at each end of next row and fol 3 alt rows. (11 sts.)
Work 31 rows.
Dec 1 st at each end of next row and fol 3 alt rows. (3 sts.)
P 1 row.
Cast off.

HEAD

Cast on 9 sts and work 2 rows.
Next row: Inc in first st, k to last st, inc in last st.
Next row: Inc in first st, p to end.
Rep last 2 rows three times more. (21 sts.)
Place markers at each end of last row.

Next row: K2tog, k to last 2 sts, k2tog.
Next row: P2tog, p to end.
Rep last 2 rows three times more. (9 sts.)
Cast off.
Work another side to match this one, rev shapings.

HEAD GUSSET

Work as for body gusset but work 21 rows without shaping.

LEGS (make 4)

Cast on 18 sts and work 4 rows.
Next row: K5, (k2tog) 4 times, k5. (14 sts.)
Work 15 rows, beg with p row.
Cast off.

SOLES (make 4)

Cast on 3 sts and work 2 rows.
Next row: Inc 1 st at each end.
Work 3 rows.
Dec 1 st at each end of next row. (3 sts.)
P 1 row.
Cast off.

TAIL

Cast on 12 sts and work 36 rows.
Next row: * K2tog, rep from * to end.
Next row: P to end. Rep last 2 rows once more. Thread yarn through rem 3 sts, draw up, and secure.

EARS (make 4)

Cast on 9 sts and work 6 rows.
Dec 1 st at each end of next row and fol 2 alt rows.
Next row: P3tog; fasten off.

TO MAKE UP

Stitch body gusset to lower edge of body from cast-on to cast-off edge. Stitch rem body sides, leaving neck open. Fill. Stitch head gusset to top of head, between markers. Stitch rem head edges, leaving cast-on edge open for neck. Fill; stitch to body. Stitch side seams of legs, stitch soles to cast-on edges, fill, and stitch to body. Stitch side edges of tail tog, fill, and stitch to body. Stitch ears tog in pairs; stitch to head. Cut out eyes; stitch to face. Embroider features. Tie bow.

PRUNELLA PERSIAN

MATERIALS
Approx 100 g (4 oz) mohair in grey and a small ball of DK yarn in black for features; one pair of 3.75 mm (No. 9) knitting needles; polyester filling; small pieces of felt in yellow for eyes; 1 m (1 yd) ribbon.

LENGTH
Approx 24 cm (9 in).

ABBREVIATIONS
See page 7.

Note: entire cat is worked in rev st st, and in grey.

BODY (make 2)
Cast on 15 sts and work 2 rows rev st st, beg with p row.
Inc 1 st at each end of next row and fol 5 alt rows. (27 sts.)
Work 33 rows.
Dec 1 st at each end of next row and fol 5 alt rows. (15 sts.)
K 1 row.
Cast off.

HEAD (make 2)
Cast on 11 sts and work 2 rows rev st st, beg with p row.
Next row: Inc in first st, p to last st, inc in last st.
Next row: Inc in first st, k to end.
Rep last 2 rows three times more. (23 sts.) Place markers at each end of last row.
Work 8 rows.
Next row: P2tog, p to last 2 sts, p2tog.
Next row: K2tog, k to end.
Rep last 2 rows three times more. (11 sts.)
Cast off.

HEAD GUSSET
Cast on 3 sts and work 2 rows rev st st, beg with p row.
Inc 1 st at each end of next row and fol 3 alt rows. (11 sts.)
Work 15 rows.

Dec 1 st at each end of next row and fol 3 alt rows. (3 sts.)
Work 1 row.
Cast off.

FEET (make 2)
Cast on 20 sts and work 16 rows rev st st, beg with p row.
Next row: * P2tog, rep from * to end.
Next row: K to end.
Rep last 2 rows once more. (5 sts.)
Thread yarn through sts, draw up, and fasten off.

TAIL
Make as for a foot but work 40 rows before shaping.

EARS (make 4)
Cast on 9 sts and work 8 rows rev st st, beg with p row.
Dec 1 st at each end of next row and fol 2 alt rows.
Next row: K3tog; fasten off.

TO MAKE UP
Stitch body sections tog, leaving cast-off edges open for filling. Fill and close. Stitch head gusset to top of head, between markers. Stitch rem head edges, leaving cast-on edges open for neck. Fill and place head at one end of body so that the face looks to the side and the body seams are on the sides. Stitch head to body. Stitch side and cast-off edges of feet and tail, fill, and stitch to respective ends, as in photograph. Secure tail to body so that it curves round the body towards front. Stitch ears tog in pairs and stitch to head. Cut out eyes and stitch to face. Embroider nose, mouth and whiskers and a pupil in each eye. Tie bow.

MARTIN MOUSE

MATERIALS
Approx 50 g (2 oz) each of DK in blue and white; a small ball of the same yarn in black for features and mauve for scarf; one pair 3.75 mm (No. 9) knitting needles; polyester filling; small pieces of felt in black and white for eyes.

LENGTH
Approx 45 cm (18 in).

ABBREVIATIONS
See page 7.

Note: entire mouse is worked in gst.

BODY (make 2)
Begin at leg
* Using W, cast on 13 sts and k 12 rows.
Change to BL and k 24 rows. *
Break off yarn and leave sts on a spare N.
Work second leg
Work from * to *.
Next row: Using W, k across sts for second leg, then k across sts for first leg. (26 sts.)
K 46 rows.
Cast off.

ARMS (make 2)
Using W, cast on 22 sts and k 10 rows.
Change to BL and k 22 rows.
Cast off.

HEAD (make 2)
Using BL, cast on 12 sts and k 1 row.
Inc 1 st at each end of next 7 rows. (26 sts.)
K 26 rows.
Dec 1 st at each end of next 7 rows. (12 sts.)
Cast off.

MUZZLE
Using W, cast on 11 sts and k 3 rows.
Next row: Inc 1 st at each end.

K 10 rows.
Dec 1 st at each end of next row and fol 2 alt rows. (5 sts.)
Cast off.

TAIL
Using BL, cast on 6 sts and k 50 rows.
Cast off.

EARS (make 4)
Using BL, cast on 16 sts and k 18 rows.
Dec 1 st at each end of next 4 rows. (8 sts.)
Cast off.

CLAWS (make 4)
Using B, cast on 8 sts and k 1 row.
Next row: Cast off 4 sts, k to end.
Next row: K4, cast on 4 sts.
Next 2 rows: K to end.
Rep last 4 rows four times more. (8 sts.)
Cast off.

SCARF
Using M, cast on 10 sts and k 220 rows.
Cast off.

TO MAKE UP
Stitch side seams of legs and body and inner leg seams. Stitch claws to cast-on edges. Stitch shoulders, leaving approx 5 cm (2 in) open for neck, and fill. Stitch side seams of arms and stitch claws to cast-on edges. Fill and stitch to body. Stitch head sections tog, leaving cast-on edge open for neck. Fill and stitch to body. Stitch muzzle to face, matching cast-off edges as in photograph, filling lightly. Stitch ears tog in pairs and stitch cast-on edges to head. Stitch side edges of tail and stitch to body. Cut eyes from felt and stitch to face. Embroider features. Cut 28 x 8 cm (3¼ in) pieces of M yarn and make fringes along cast-on and cast-off edges of scarf.

WALLY WABBIT

MATERIALS

Approx 100 g (4 oz) of DK in pink, 50 g (2 oz) of same yarn in white, and a small ball in black; one pair 3.75 mm (No. 9) knitting needles; polyester filling; small pieces of felt in black and white for eyes; 1 m (1 yd) ribbon.

LENGTH

Approx 50 cm (20 in).

ABBREVIATIONS

See page 7.

Note: entire rabbit is worked in gst.

LEGS (make 2)

Using PK, cast on 26 sts and k 1 row.
Inc 1 st at each end of next 2 rows. (30 sts.)
K 11 rows.
Dec 1 st at each end of next 4 rows. (22 sts.)
K 20 rows.
Cast off.

ARMS (make 2)

Using PK, cast on 12 sts and k 1 row.
Next row: Inc in first st, k4, inc in next 2 sts, k4, inc in last st.
K 1 row.
Next row: Inc in first st, k6, inc in next 2 sts, k6, inc in last st. (20 sts.)
K 28 rows.
Cast off.

BODY (make 2)

Using PK, cast on 14 sts and k 1 row.
Cast on 3 sts at beg of next 4 rows. (26 sts.)
K 4 rows.
Change to W and k 32 rows.
Change to PK and k 4 rows.
Cont using PK and cast off 3 sts at beg of next 4 rows. (14 sts.)
Cast off.

HEAD (make 2)

Using PK, cast on 12 sts and k 1 row.
Inc 1 st at each end of next 7 rows. (26 sts.)
K 26 rows.
Dec 1 st at each end of next 7 rows. (12 sts.)
Cast off.

MUZZLE (make 2)

Using W, cast on 11 sts and k 12 rows.
Dec 1 st at each end of next 4 rows. (3 sts.)
Cast off.

EARS (make 2 PK and 2 W)

Cast on 16 sts and k 40 rows.
Dec 1 st at each end of next row and fol 4 alt rows. (6 sts.)
Cast off.

TO MAKE UP

Stitch side seams and cast-on edges of legs and arms and fill. Stitch body sections tog, leaving cast-off edges open for neck. Fill. Stitch head sections, leaving cast-on edges open for neck. Fill and stitch to body. Stitch side and cast-off edges of muzzle. Fill and stitch to face. Stitch ears tog in pairs and stitch to head. Fold tops of legs so that toes point to the front and stitch to body. Stitch arms to body.

Embroider features and cut out eyes, and stitch to face. Tie bow. Make a pompon (see page 60) using W and stitch to back for a tail.

BARRY BUNNY

MATERIALS
Approx 75 g (3 oz) of DK in pink, 25 g (1 oz) of the same yarn in white; a length of black yarn for features; one pair 3.75 mm (No. 9) knitting needles; polyester filling.

LENGTH
Approx 20 cm (8 in).

ABBREVIATIONS
See page 7.

BODY AND HEAD
Using PK, cast on 6 sts.
Next row: Inc in each st.
(12 sts.)
P 1 row.
Next row: * K1, inc in next st, rep from * to end.
P 1 row.
Next row: * K2, inc in next st, rep from * to end. (24 sts.)
P 1 row.
Next row: * K3, inc in next st, rep from * to end. (30 sts.)
Work 17 rows st st, beg with p row.
Next row: K4, inc in next st, rep from * to end.
P 1 row.
Next row: * K5, inc in next st, rep from * to end. (42 sts.)
P 1 row.
Next row: * K6, inc in next st, rep from * to end. (48 sts.)
Work 27 rows st st, beg with p row.
Next row: * K4, k2tog, rep from * to end.
P 1 row.
Next row: * K3, k2tog, rep from * to end. (32 sts.)
Next row: P to end.
Next row: * K2, k2tog, rep from * to end.
P 1 row.
Next row: * K1, k2tog, rep from * to end. (16 sts.)
P 1 row.
Next row: (K2tog) 8 times.
Thread yarn through rem sts, draw up and secure.

GUSSET
Using PK, cast on 3 sts and work 4 rows st st.
Cont in st st and inc 1 st at each end of next row and every fourth row until 11 sts on N.
Work 31 rows st st, beg with p row.
Dec 1 st at each end of next row and every fourth row until 3 sts rem.
Work 3 rows st st, beg with p row.
Next row: K3tog; fasten off.

EARS (make 2 PK and 2 W)
Cast on 11 sts and work 20 rows st st.
Cont in st st and dec 1 st at each end of next row and fol 2 alt rows. (5 sts.)
P 1 row.
Cast off.

FRONT FEET (make 2)
Using PK, cast on 14 sts and work 10 rows st st.
Next row: (K2tog) 7 times.
Thread yarn through rem 7 sts, draw up, and secure.

TO MAKE UP
Stitch gusset to sides of body, thus forming a base, leaving approx 5 cm (2 in) open for filling. Fill and close. Stitch side edges of feet, fill and stitch to body as shown in the photograph. Stitch ears tog in pairs and stitch securely to top of head. Make a pompon (see page 60) from W for tail and stitch into position. Embroider features using B, as shown in photograph.

CLARENCE CLOWN

MATERIALS
50 g (2 oz) each of DK in blue and red and small balls of the same yarn in black, white, green and yellow; one pair 3.75 mm (No. 9) knitting needles; polyester filling; small pieces of felt in black, pink and red for features.

HEIGHT
Approx 48 cm (19 in).

ABBREVIATIONS
See page 7.

BODY AND LEGS
Using R, cast on 20 sts.
Next row: Inc in each st. (40 sts.)
Work 75 rows st st, beg with p row, placing markers at each end of 26th row for crotch.
Cast off.
Using BL, work another piece to match.

ARMS (make 1 R and 1 BL)
Cast on 16 sts.
Next row: Inc in each st. (32 sts.)
Work 27 rows st st, beg with p row.
Cast off.

HEAD (make 2)
Using W, cast on 14 sts and work 2 rows st st.
Cont in st st and inc 1 st at each end of next row and fol 5 alt rows. (26 sts.)
Work 7 rows st st, beg with p row.
Cont in st st and dec 1 st at each end of next row and fol 5 alt rows. (14 sts.)
P 1 row.
Cast off.

HANDS (make 2)
Using W, cast on 18 sts and work 8 rows st st.
Cast off 2 sts at beg of next 2 rows. (14 sts.)
Work 4 rows st st.
Next row: K2tog, k3, (k2tog) twice, k3, k2tog. (10 sts.)
Cast off.

FEET (make 2)
Using B, cast on 40 sts.
Next row: Inc in first st, k18, inc in next 2 sts, k18, inc in last st. (44 sts.)
Work 7 rows st st, beg with p row.
Dec 1 st at each end of next 2 rows.
Cast off 10 sts at beg of next 2 rows. (20 sts.)
Work 2 rows st st.
Cast off.

HAIR
Using Y, cast on 41 sts and k 1 row.
Next row: * K1, k next st in the usual way but do not slip st off LHN. Insert RHN into back of same st, wind yarn around first and second fingers at back of work, then complete st, slipping original st off N at same time. Yon and pass st (both loops) over the yon. Rep from * to last st, k1.
Rep last 2 rows three times more.
Cast off.

FRILLS
LEGS (make 1 R and 1 BL)
Cast on 50 sts and k 6 rows.
Next row: * K2tog, rep from * to end. (25 sts.)
Cast off.

WRISTS (make 1 R and 1 BL)
Cast on 44 sts and work as for leg frills.

NECK
Using BL, cast on 100 sts and k 6 rows.
Next row: * K2tog, rep from * to end.
Rep last row once more. (25 sts.)
Cast off.

HAT
Using GR, cast on 52 sts and k 4 rows.
Work 8 rows st st.
Next row: * K2, k2tog, rep from * to end.
Work 5 rows st st, beg with p row.
Next row: * K1, k2tog, rep from * to end. (26 sts.)
Work 5 rows st st, beg with p row.
Next row: * K2tog, rep from * to end. (13 sts.)
Work 3 rows st st, beg with p row.
Next row: * K2tog, rep from * to last st, k1.
Thread yarn through rem sts, draw up, and secure.

NOSE
Using R, cast on 5 sts and work 2 rows st st.
Next row: Inc 1 st at each end.
Work 5 rows st st, beg with p row.
Dec 1 st at each end of next row. (5 sts.)
P 1 row. Cast off.

TO MAKE UP
Fold legs in half and stitch side seams up to crotch markers. Stitch these two sections tog at centre front and centre back, to form body. Stitch cast-off edges for shoulders, leaving approx 5 cm (2 in) open at middle for neck. Stitch cast-on edges, side and first 10 sts of cast-off edges of shoes tog; fill and stitch to cast-on edges of legs. Fill body. Stitch side edges of arms. Stitch side edges of hands, fill and stitch to cast-on edges of arms. Fill arms and stitch to body. Stitch head sections tog, leaving cast-on edges open for neck; fill and stitch to body. Run a gathering thread along edges of nose, draw up, fill, and stitch to face. Stitch hair to head. Stitch side edges of hat. Fold approx 1 cm (1/2 in) of lower edge of hat up to form a small brim, fill the hat lightly to retain shape and stitch to head. Stitch frills round neck, wrists and legs. Cut eyes, cheeks, and mouth from black, pink and red felt and stitch neatly to face. Using B, stitch lines across eyes as shown in the photograph. Make three pompons (see page 60) using GR and stitch down centre front. Make one pompon using R and stitch to hat.

ORPHAN ANNIE

MATERIALS
Approx 50 g (2 oz) each of DK in pink, red, yellow and white; small balls of same yarn in black and blue; one pair 3.75 mm (No. 9) knitting needles; polyester filling; small pieces of felt in white, blue and red for features; crochet hook.

HEIGHT
Approx 38 cm (15 in).

ABBREVIATIONS
See page 7.

BODY (make 2)
Using B, cast on 22 sts.
Next row: K10, inc in next 2 sts, k10.
P 1 row.
Next row: K11, inc in next 2 sts, k11.
P 1 row.
Next row: K12, inc in next 2 sts, k12. (28 sts.)
Work 3 rows st st, beg with p row.
Next row: K12, (k2tog) twice, k12.
P 1 row.
Next row: K11, (k2tog) twice, k11.
P 1 row.
Next row: K10, (k2tog) twice, k10. (22 sts.)
P 1 row.
Change to PK and work 24 rows st st.
Cont in st st, and cast on 2 sts at beg of next 2 rows. (26 sts.)
Work 18 rows st st.
Change to R and work 20 rows st st.
Cast off.

ARMS (make 2)
Using PK, cast on 8 sts.
Next row: Inc in first st, k2, inc in next 2 sts, k2, inc in last st. (12 sts.)
P 1 row.
Next row: Inc in first st, k4, inc in next 2 sts, k4, inc in last st.
P 1 row.
Next row: Inc in first st, k6, inc in next 2 sts, k6, inc in last st. (20 sts.)
P 1 row.
Work 12 rows st st.

Change to R and k 4 rows.
Work 8 rows st st.
Cast off.

HEAD (make 2)
Using PK, cast on 10 sts and work 2 rows st st.
Cont in st st and inc 1 st at each end of next row and fol 3 alt rows. (18 sts.) Place markers at each end of last row.
Work 6 rows st st.
Dec 1 st at each end of next row and fol 3 alt rows. (10 sts.) Cast off.

HEAD GUSSET
Using PK, cast on 2 sts and work 2 rows st st.
Next row: Inc in both sts.
P 1 row.
Inc 1 st at each end of next row and fol alt row. (8 sts.)
Work 29 rows st st, beg with p row.
Dec 1 st at each end of next row and fol 2 alt rows. (2 sts.)
Work 2 rows st st. Cast off.

SKIRT
Using R, cast on 104 sts and k 8 rows.
Next row: P to end.
Change to BL and work 2 rows st st.
Change to R and work 2 rows st st.
Change to BL and work 2 rows st st.
Change to R and work 24 rows st st.
Next row: (K2tog) 52 times.
K 3 rows.
Cast off.

SCARF (make 2)
Using W, cast on 50 sts and k 2 rows.
Next row: K1, k2tog, k to last 3 sts, k2tog, k1.
Rep last row until 4 sts rem.
Next row: K1, k2tog, k1.
Next row: K3tog; fasten off.

NOSE
Using PK, cast on 5 sts and work 2 rows st st.
Next row: Inc 1 st at each end.
P 1 row.

Dec 1 st at each end of next row. (5 sts.)
P 1 row. Cast off.

PANTIES
Using W, cast on 54 sts and k 4 rows.
Work 14 rows st st.
Work 4 rows k1, p1 rib. Cast off.

BROOCH
Using Y, cast on 3 sts and k 1 row.
Next row: K, inc 1 st at each end.
K 1 row.
Dec 1 st at each end of next row. (3 sts.) Cast off.

TO MAKE UP
Stitch inner leg seams to crotch, then stitch body pieces tog down centre front and back. Fill. Stitch across cast-off edges to form shoulders, leaving 5 cm (2 in) open at centre for neck. Stitch head gusset to top of head, beg and end at markers. Stitch rem edges tog, leaving cast-on edges open for neck. Fill and stitch to body. Fold arms in half lengthwise, stitch, fill and attach to upper body. Cut 90 lengths of Y yarn approx 30 cm (12 in) long and stitch to centre of head to form hair. Tie in bunches at side of face and secure. Make a fringe by threading six pieces of Y through seams at top of head. Run a thread round edges of nose and draw up to form a ball. Fill and stitch to face. Cut eyes and mouth from felt and stitch to face. Embroider eyelashes and use a little lipstick for cheek colour. Stitch back seam of panties tog, and secure a small section of cast-on edge tog to form crotch. Stitch back seam of skirt and slip-stitch cast-off edge round waist to secure. Stitch approx 9 cm (3½ in) of cast-on edge of scarf to form back. Lap corners over each other at front waist and secure. Embroider a 'jewel' using B in centre of brooch and stitch brooch to corners of scarf. Using B, crochet a length of chain and tie round neck.

PEPPI PIERROT

MATERIALS
Approx 75 g (3 oz) each of DK in black and white; one pair 3.75 mm (No. 9) knitting needles; polyester filling; small pieces of felt in black and red for features.

HEIGHT
Approx 55 cm (21 in).

ABBREVIATIONS
See page 7.

BODY AND LEGS
Using B, cast on 24 sts and work 88 rows st st. Place markers at each end of 60th row for crotch.
Change to W and work 20 rows st st.
Cast off.
Work another piece to match, rev the cols.

ARMS (make 1 B and 1 W)
Cast on 15 sts.
Next row: *K2, inc in next st, rep from * to end. (20 sts.)
Work 37 rows st st beg with p row.
Cast off.

HEAD (make 2)
Using W, cast on 12 sts and work 2 rows st st.
Cont in st st and inc 1 st at each end of next row and fol 4 alt rows.
(22 sts.)
Work 7 rows st st, beg with p row.
Dec 1 st at each end of next row and fol 4 alt rows. (12 sts.)
P 1 row.
Cast off.

SHOES (make 2)
Using B, cast on 28 sts.
Next row: K13, inc in next 2 sts, k13. (30 sts.)
Work 5 rows st st, beg with p row.
Next row: K11, (k2tog) 4 times, k11.
Next row: P9, (p2tog) 4 times, p9. (22 sts.)
Cast off.

HANDS (make 2)
Using W, cast on 7 sts.
Next row: Inc in each st. (14 sts.)
Work 5 rows st st beg with p row.
Cast on 3 sts at beg of next 2 rows. (20 sts.)
Work 3 rows st st.
Next row: * P2, p2tog, rep from * to end. (15 sts.)
Cast off.

NECK FRILLS (make 1 W and 1 B)
Cast on 100 sts and k 6 rows.
Next row: (K2tog) 50 times.
Next row: (K2tog) 25 times. (25 sts.)
Cast off.

HAT
Using B, cast on 40 sts and k 4 rows.
Work 6 rows st st.
Next row: * K2, K2tog, rep from * to end.
Work 3 rows st st, beg with p row.
Next row: * K1, k2tog, rep from * to end. (20 sts.)
Work 3 rows st st, beg with p row.
Next row: * K2tog, rep from * to end.
Rep last 4 rows once more. (5 sts.)
Thread yarn through rem sts, draw up, and secure.

TO MAKE UP
Fold legs in half and stitch seams up to crotch markers. Stitch body sections tog at centre front and centre back. Stitch cast-off edges tog to form shoulders, leaving approx 4 cm (1½ in) open at middle for neck. Stitch side and cast-on edges of shoes, fill, and stitch to legs. Fill legs and body. Stitch side seams of arms. Stitch cast-on and side seams of hands, fill, and stitch to cast-on edges of arms. Fill arms and stitch to body. Stitch head sections, leaving cast-on edges open for neck. Fill, and stitch to body. Stitch cast-off edges of frills tog, place around neck and stitch respective side edges. Stitch side edge of hat, fill lightly to keep shape, and slip-stitch to head. Make three pompons using both cols as follows: cut two circles of cardboard slightly bigger than pompon required. Cut a hole approx 1 cm (½ in) in diameter in centre of each. Wind yarn evenly around two circles. Cut yarn between circles at outer edge and open slightly. Secure cut pieces at centre, between circles, with a matching piece of yarn. Stitch one pompon to top of hat and one of the others to each shoe. Cut eyes and mouth from black and red felt and stitch to face. Using B, stitch lines across eyes.

WILSON WHALE

MATERIALS
Approx 75 g (3 oz) each of DK in black and white; one pair 3.75 mm (No. 9) knitting needles; polyester filling; small pieces of felt in black and white for eyes.

LENGTH
Approx 35 cm (14 in).

ABBREVIATIONS
See page 7.

BODY (make 2 B and 1 W)
Cast on 3 sts and work 3 rows st st. Inc 1 st at each end of next row and fol 6 alt rows. (17 sts.)

Cont in st st and inc 1 st at each end of every fourth row until 27 sts on N. Work 12 rows st st.
Dec 1 st at each end of next row and on every fol fourth row until 9 sts rem.
Dec 1 st at each end of every alt row until 3 sts rem.
Cast off.

FINS (make 4 B and 4 W)
Cast on 9 sts and k 1 row.
Next row: Inc in first st, k to end.
Next row: K to end.
Next row: Inc in first st, k to end.
Next row: K2tog, k to end.
Rep last 4 rows five times more. (15 sts.)
Cast off.

GILL FLAPS (make 2)
Using W, cast on 8 sts.
Next row: Inc in first st, k to end.
Next row: K2tog, k to end.
Rep last 2 rows six times more.
Cast off.

TO MAKE UP
Stitch side edges of body sections tog, leaving approx 5 cm (2 in) open at centre for filling. Fill body and close seam. Stitch cast-off edges of two pairs of fins tog and then stitch tog to form tail. Stitch to cast-off end of body. Stitch rem fins tog in pairs and stitch to body as in photograph. Cut eyes from felt and stitch to face. Stitch gill flaps in position behind eyes.

DILLYS DOLPHIN

MATERIALS

Approx 70 g (3 oz) DK in blue; 25 g (1 oz) of same yarn in white; one pair 3.75 mm (No. 9) knitting needles; polyester filling; pieces of felt in black and white for eyes.

LENGTH

Approx 35 cm (14 in).

ABBREVIATIONS

See page 7.

BODY (make 2 BL and 1 W)

Cast on 3 sts and work 3 rows st st.

Inc 1 st at each end of next row and fol 6 alt rows.
(17 sts.)
Cont in st st and inc 1 st at each end of every fourth row until 27 sts on N.
Work 12 rows st st.
Dec 1 st at each end of next row and on every fol fourth row until 9 sts rem.
Dec 1 st at each end of every alt row until 3 sts rem.
Cast off.

FINS (make 10)

Using BL, cast on 9 sts and k 1 row.
Next row: Inc in first st, k to end.

Next row: K to end.
Next row: Inc in first st, k to end.
Next row: K2tog, k to end.
Rep last 4 rows five times more.
(15 sts.)
Cast off.

TO MAKE UP

Stitch side edges of body sections, leaving approx 5 cm (2 in) open at centre for filling. Fill and close. Stitch cast-off edges of two pairs of fins tog and then stitch tog to form tail. Stitch to cast-off end of body. Stitch rem fins tog in pairs and stitch to body as in photograph. Cut eyes from felt and stitch to face.

OSCAR OCTOPUS

MATERIALS
Approx 30 g (1½ oz) each of DK in blue and white; one pair 3.75 mm (No. 9) knitting needles; polyester filling; small pieces of felt in black and white for eyes.

SIZE
Approx 30 cm (12 in) across, from tips of tentacles.

ABBREVIATIONS
See page 7.

BODY
Using BL, cast on 8 sts.
Next row: Inc into each st. (16 sts.)
P 1 row.
Next row: * K1, inc in next st, rep from * to end.
P 1 row.
Next row: * K2, inc in next st, rep from * to end. (32 sts.)
P 1 row.
Next row: * K3, inc in next st, rep from * to end.
P 1 row.
Next row: * K4, inc in next st, rep from * to end. (48 sts.)
Work 17 rows st st, beg with p row.
Cast off.

BASE
Using W, cast on 10 sts and work 2 rows st st.
Cont in st st and inc 1 st at each end of next row and fol 4 alt rows.
(20 sts.)
Work 7 rows st st, beg with p row.
Dec 1 st at each end of next row and fol 4 alt rows.
(10 sts.)
P 1 row.
Cast off.

TENTACLES (make 8)
Using BL, cast on 8 sts and work 30 rows st st.
Dec 1 st at each end of next 2 rows.
(4 sts.)
Cast off.

TENTACLE LININGS (make 8)
Using W, cast on 6 sts and work 30 rows st st.
Dec 1 st at each end of next row.
(4 sts.)
Cast off.

TO MAKE UP
Stitch side edges of body and stitch base to cast-off edge, leaving 5 cm (2 in) open for filling. Fill and close. Stitch tentacle linings to tentacles, fill lightly, and stitch to edge of body. Cut eyes from felt; stitch to face.

PORTIA THE BABY POLAR BEAR

MATERIALS
Approx 100 g (4 oz) DK in white; a small ball of same yarn in black for features; one pair 3.75 mm (No. 9) knitting needles; polyester filling; small pieces of felt in black and white for features; 1 m (1 yd) ribbon.

HEIGHT
30 cm (12 in).

ABBREVIATIONS
See page 7.

Note: entire bear is worked in gst. White yarn is used throughout, except for features.

LEGS (make 2)
Cast on 26 sts and k 1 row.
Inc 1 st at each end of next 2 rows. (30 sts.)
K 9 rows.
Dec 1 st at each end of next 4 rows. (22 sts.)
K 16 rows.
Cast off.

ARMS (make 2)
Cast on 12 sts and k 1 row.
Next row: Inc in first st, k4, inc in each of next 2 sts, k4, inc in last st.
K 1 row.
Next row: Inc in first st, k6, inc in each of next 2 sts, k6, inc in last st. (20 sts.)
K 24 rows.
Cast off.

BODY (make 2)
Cast on 14 sts and k 1 row.
Cast on 3 sts at beg of next 4 rows. (26 sts.)
K 40 rows.
Cast off 3 sts at beg of next 4 rows. (14 sts.)
Cast off.

HEAD (make 2)
Cast on 12 sts and k 1 row.

Inc 1 st at each end of next 7 rows. (26 sts.)
K 26 rows.
Dec 1 st at each end of next 7 rows. (12 sts.)
Cast off.

MUZZLE
Cast on 14 sts and k 8 rows.
Next row: (K2tog) 7 times. (7 sts.)
Thread yarn through rem sts, draw up, and fasten off.

EARS (make 4)
Cast on 12 sts and k 12 rows.
Dec 1 st at each end of next 4 rows.
(4 sts.)
Cast off.

TO MAKE UP
Stitch side and cast-on edges of arms and legs. Fill. Stitch body sections tog, leaving cast-off edges open for neck. Fill. Stitch head sections tog, leaving cast-on edges open for neck. Fill. Stitch head to body; stitch arms and legs to body, folding top of leg so that 'toe' points to front. Stitch ears tog in pairs; stitch to head. Stitch side of muzzle piece, leaving cast-on edge open; fill. Stitch to lower half of head. Cut out eyes and nose; stitch in place. Tie bow.

SALLY SEAL

MATERIALS
Approx 80 g (3 oz) DK in black and a small ball of the same yarn in grey for features; one pair of 3.75 mm (No. 9) knitting needles; polyester filling; small pieces of felt in black and white for eyes.

HEIGHT
Approx 28 cm (11 in).

ABBREVIATIONS
See page 7.

Note: entire seal is worked in st st, and in black, except for features.

BODY
Cast on 32 sts and work 2 rows st st.
Cont in st st and inc 1 st at each end of next row and fol 2 alt rows.
(38 sts.)
Work 4 rows st st.
Dec 1 st at beg of next row and at same edge on every fourth row until 30 sts rem, end with k row.
P 1 row.
Next row: Cast off 3 sts, k to last 2 sts, k2tog.
Next row: P to end.
Rep last 2 rows three times more, end with p row. (14 sts.) Place a marker at beg of last row.
Work 2 rows st st.
Cont in st st and inc 1 st at each end of next row and fol 6 alt rows.
(28 sts.)
Work 7 rows st st, beg with p row.
Place markers at each end of last row.
Next row: K2tog, k to end.
Next row: Cast off 2 sts, p to end.
Rep last 2 rows four times more.
(13 sts.)
Cast off.
Work another side to match this one, rev all shapings.

CHEST GUSSET
Cast on 2 sts and work 2 rows st st.
Cont in st st and inc 1 st at each end of next row and fol 3 alt rows.
(10 sts.)
Work 31 rows st st, beg with p row.
Dec 1 st at each end of next row and fol 3 alt rows.
(2 sts.)
P 1 row.
Cast off.

HEAD GUSSET
Work as for chest gusset, but work 37 rows without shaping.

FLIPPERS (make 4)
Cast on 8 sts and k 1 row.
Next row: Inc in first st, k to end.
Rep last 2 rows six times more.
(15 sts.)
Next row: K to end.
Next row: K2tog, k to end.
Rep last 2 rows six times more.
(8 sts.)
Cast off loosely.

TAIL FLIPPERS (make 2)
Cast on 20 sts and k 1 row.
Next row: K2tog, k to end.

Rep last 2 rows eight times more.
(11 sts.)
K 3 rows.
Next row: Inc in first st, k to end.
Next row: K to end.
Rep last 2 rows eight times more.
(20 sts.)
Cast off loosely.

TO MAKE UP
Stitch body gusset to relevant edges of body sections from beg of cast-on edge to marker at neck. Stitch head gusset to top of head between markers. Stitch rem edges, leaving approx 5 cm (2 in) open at back for filling. Fill and close. Stitch flippers tog in pairs, leaving straight side edge open, fill lightly, and stitch to lower front of body, gathering slightly. Stitch tail flipper sections tog, leaving straight side edge open, fill lightly, and stitch to end of body, gathering slightly. Cut eyes from black and white felt and stitch to face.
   Embroider nose and whiskers using G yarn.

LACY SET FOR BABY DOLL

MATERIALS
100 g (4 oz) of 4 ply in white (or colour of your choice); one pair each 3 mm (No. 11) and 3.25 mm (No. 10) knitting needles; one 2.5 mm (No. 12) crochet hook; 4 small buttons; shirring elastic.

SIZE
To fit a baby doll approx 38 cm (15 in) in height.

TENSION
26 sts and 33 rows to 10 cm (4 in) over stocking stitch, using 3 mm (No. 11) Ns.

ABBREVIATIONS
See page 7.

DRESS
Begin with skirt
Using 3.25 mm (No. 10) Ns, cast on 114 sts and k 3 rows. Cont in patt as follows:
Row 1: K to end.
Rows 2, 4: P to end.
Row 3: K2,* yrn, p1, p3tog, p1, yon, k2, rep from * to end.
Rep these 4 rows for patt.
Cont in patt until the work measures 13 cm (5 in) from beg, ending with fourth row.
Next row: K2tog, * k2, k2tog, rep from * to end. (85 sts.)
Change to 3 mm (No. 11) Ns. Work 5 rows st st, beg with p row.
Divide for armholes
Next row: K18, cast off 7, k35, cast off 7, k18.
Work on these last 18 sts for right back.
Work 21 rows st st, beg with p row. Cast off.

Rejoin yarn to middle section and work front as follows:
Work 11 rows st st, beg with p row.
Shape neck
Next row: K13, cast off 9, k13. Work on these last sts only for first side.

Dec 1 st at neck edge on next 4 rows. (9 sts.)
Cont straight until same no. of rows worked as for back to shoulder.
Cast off.

Rejoin yarn to rem sts and work to match first side, rev shapings.

Rejoin yarn to sts for left back. Work 21 rows st st, beg with p row.
Cast off.

SLEEVES (make 2)
Using 3 mm (No. 11) Ns, cast on 20 sts and k 2 rows.
Next row: * K1, inc in next st, rep from * to end. (30 sts.)
Change to 3.25 mm (No. 10) Ns and work 16 rows patt as for skirt.
Cast off.

NECKBAND
Stitch both shoulders. Using 3 mm (No. 11) Ns, pick up and k 48 sts evenly round neck.
K 3 rows. Cast off.

HAT
Using 3.25 mm (No. 10) Ns, cast on 64 sts and k 3 rows.
Cont in patt with gst borders as fols:
Row 1: K3, patt as for skirt to last 3 sts, k3.
Rep this row while working patt until 20 patt rows completed.
Shape crown
Next row: * K2tog, k2, rep from * to end.
K 3 rows.
Next row: * K2tog, k1, rep from * to end. (32 sts.)
K 3 rows.
Next row: * K2tog, rep from * to end.
Next row: K to end.
Rep last 2 rows once more. (8 sts.)
Thread yarn through sts, draw up, and secure.

BOOTEES (make 2)

Using 3 mm (No. 11) Ns, cast on 25 sts.

Next row: Inc in first st, k10, inc in next st, k1, inc in next st, k10, inc in last st.

K 1 row.

Next row: Inc in first st, k12, inc in next st, k1, inc in next st, k12, inc in last st.

(33 sts.)

K 8 rows.

Next row: K14, k2tog, k1, k2tog, k14.

Next row: K14, k2tog, k15.

(30 sts.)

Change to 3.25 mm (No. 10) Ns and work 12 rows patt as for skirt.

K 4 rows.

Cast off loosely.

PANTIES (make 2)

Using 3.25 mm (No. 10) Ns, cast on 35 sts and k 3 rows.

Work 4 rows st st.

Cont in st st and cast on 4 sts at beg of next 2 rows. (43 sts.)

Work 24 rows st st, dec 1 st at centre of last row.

Change to 3 mm (No. 11) Ns and work 6 rows k1, p1 rib.

Cast off loosely ribwise.

TO MAKE UP

DRESS

Stitch skirt to within 2 cm (3/4 in) of waist. Stitch sleeve seam, leaving 1 cm (1/2 in) open at top for armhole. Stitch sleeves into armholes. Using 2.5 mm (No. 12) crochet hook, work 2 rows dc round both sides of back opening, working 4 x 3-chain button loops, evenly placed along right back edge. Sew on buttons.

HAT

Stitch back seam from centre to end of crown shapings. Using crochet hook make 2 x 12-cm (4 3/4-in) chains and stitch to cast-on corners for ties.

BOOTEES

Stitch side and sole seams. Make 2 x 24-cm (9 1/2-in) chains and thread them through holes formed in third patt row.

PANTIES

Stitch leg seams. Stitch crotch seam. Thread shirring elastic through rib at top of panties.

TRACKSUIT FOR BABY DOLL

MATERIALS
100 g (4 oz) 4 ply in blue and a small ball of the same yarn in white; one pair each 2.75 mm (No. 12) and 3 mm (No. 11) knitting needles; a small length of narrow elastic; 4 buttons.

SIZE
See page 68.

TENSION
See page 68.

ABBREVIATIONS
See page 7.

LEGGINGS
RIGHT LEG
Start at foot
Using 3 mm (No. 11) Ns and BL, cast on 30 sts.
Next row: K6, inc in next st, k1, inc in next st, k12, inc in next st, k1, inc in next st, k6.
K 1 row.
Next row: K7, inc in next st, k1, inc in next st, k14, inc in next st, k1, inc in next st, k7.
(38 sts.)
K 8 rows.
Next row: K8, k2tog, k1, k2tog, k25.
Next row: K24, k2tog, k1, k2tog, k7. (34 sts.)
Next row: K6, k2tog, k1, k2tog, k23. (32 sts.) *
** Work 8 rows st st.
Next row: K, inc 1 st at each end.
Work 7 rows st st, beg with p row.
Rep last 8 rows three times more. (40 sts.)
Cast on 2 sts at beg of next 2 rows.
(44 sts.)
Work 30 rows st st.
Change to 2.75 mm (No. 12) Ns and work 8 rows k1, p1 rib.
Cast off loosely ribwise.

LEFT LEG
Work as for right leg to *.

Next row: K to end.
Complete as from ** to end.

TOP (main section worked in one piece to armhole)
Using 2.75 mm (No. 12) Ns and BL, cast on 84 sts and work 8 rows k1, p1 rib. Change to 3 mm (No. 11) Ns and cont in stripe patt as fols:
Work 2 rows st st.
Change to W and work 2 rows st st.
Change to BL and work 2 rows st st.
Change to W and work 2 rows st st.
Change to BL and work 2 rows st st.
Divide for armholes
Next row: K17, cast off 7, k36, cast off 7, k17. Work on these last sts only for right back.
Work 23 rows st st, beg with p row.
Cast off.

Rejoin yarn to centre group of sts and work front as follows:
Work 13 rows st st, beg with p row.
Divide for neck
Next row: K13, cast off 10, k13. Work on these last sts only for first side. Dec 1 st at neck edge on next

3 rows.
(10 sts.)
Cont straight until same no. of rows worked as for back to shoulder.
Cast off.

Rejoin yarn to rem sts and work to match first side, rev shapings.

Rejoin yarn to sts for left back and work 23 rows st st, beg with p row.
Cast off.

SLEEVES (make 2)
Using 2.75 mm (No. 12) Ns and BL, cast on 24 sts and work 7 rows k1, p1 rib.
Next row: Rib 4, * m1, rib 3, rep from * to last 5 sts, m1, rib 5.
(30 sts.)
Change to 3 mm (No. 11) Ns and work stripe patt as for first 8 rows of main section.
Cont in st st, using BL only for 16 rows.
Cast off.

NECKBAND
Stitch shoulder seams. Using 2.75 mm (No. 12) Ns and BL, pick up and k 50 sts evenly round neck.
K 3 rows and cast off loosely.

BUTTON BAND
Using 3 mm (No. 11) Ns and BL, cast on 5 sts and cont in gst until band is long enough to fit along back opening. Cast off.

BUTTONHOLE BAND
Stitch button band to relevant side and mark positions for buttonholes as follows: the first, 0.5 mm (¼ in) from cast-on edge and the last, 0.5 cm (¼ in) from cast-off edge, and two more spaced evenly between them.

Work buttonhole band as for button band but make buttonholes to correspond with markers as follows:
Next row: K2, yf, k2tog, k1.

HAT
Using 2.75 mm (No. 12) Ns and BL, cast on 64 sts and work 8 rows k1, p1 rib. Change to 3 mm (No. 11) Ns and work 8 rows stripe patt as for main section of top. Work 16 rows st st using BL only.
Shape top
Next row: * K2, k2tog, rep from * to end.
P 1 row.
Next row: * K1, k2tog, rep from * to end.
(32 sts.)
P 1 row.
Next row: (K2tog) 16 times.
P 1 row.
Next row: (K2tog) 8 times.
(8 sts.)
Thread yarn through sts, draw up, and secure.

TO MAKE UP
LEGGINGS
Stitch side seams of legs. Fold legs so that side seam is at inner leg and stitch cast-on edges tog for foot. Stitch crotch seams. Fold ribbing over to WS to form hem and slip-stitch in place. Thread elastic through hem.

TOP
Stitch sleeve seam, leaving 1 cm (½ in) open at top for armhole. Stitch sleeves into armholes. Stitch buttonhole band to relevant back edge. Sew on buttons. Embroider motif in duplicate stitch as per graph.

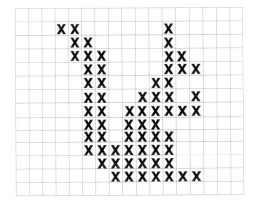

HAT
Stitch side edges of hat tog. Using W, make a small pompon (see page 60) and stitch to top.

PLAYSET FOR BABY DOLL

MATERIALS
Approx 50 g (2 oz) of 4 ply in yellow; a length of the same yarn in blue for embroidery; one pair each 2.75 mm (No. 12) and 3 mm (No. 11) knitting needles; 5 press studs; shirring elastic.

SIZE
See page 68.

TENSION
See page 68.

ABBREVIATIONS
See page 7.

MAIN SECTION
Using 2.75 mm (No. 12) Ns, cast on 40 sts and work 4 rows k1, p1 rib.
Change to 3 mm (No. 11) Ns and st st and inc 1 st at each end of next row and fol 2 alt rows.
(46 sts.)
P 1 row.
Place markers at each end of last row for crotch.
Work 12 rows st st.
Shape opening
Next row: Cast off 2 sts, k to end.
Work 39 rows st st, beg with p row.
Shape armholes
Next row: K20, cast off 4 sts, k20.
Work on the last 20 sts only for back.
Work 21 rows st st, beg with p row.
Cast off.

Rejoin yarn to rem sts at armhole and work front as follows:
Work 11 rows st st, beg with p row.
Shape neck
Next row: Cast off 4 sts, k to end.
Cont in st st and cast off 2 sts at neck edge on next 2 RS rows.
(12 sts.)
Cont without shaping until same no. of rows worked as for back to shoulder.
Cast off.
Work another piece to match first piece, rev opening and neck shaping.

SLEEVES
Using 2.75 mm (No. 12) Ns, cast on 32 sts and work 4 rows k1, p1 rib.
Change to 3 mm (No. 11) Ns and work 12 rows st st. Cast off.

FRONT BAND
With RS facing, using 2.75 mm (No.12) Ns, pick up and k 42 sts from beg of opening to neck.
Work 3 rows k1, p1 rib.
Cast off loosely ribwise.
Work a band to match on other side.

NECKBAND
Stitch shoulder seams. Stitch back seam from crotch to neck.
With RS facing, using 2.75 mm (No. 12) Ns, pick up and k 48 sts evenly around neck and across sides of bands.
Work 3 rows k1, p1 rib.
Cast off loosely ribwise.

SOCKS (make 2)
Using 3 mm (No. 12) Ns, cast on 25 sts.
Next row: Inc in first st, k10, inc in next st, k 1, inc in next st, k10, inc in last st.
K 1 row.
Next row: Inc in first st, k12, inc in next st, k1, inc in next st, k12, inc in last st. (33 sts.)

K 8 rows.
Next row: K14, k2tog, k1, k2tog, k 14.
Next row: K 13, k2tog, k1, k2tog, k13. (29 sts.)
Work 12 rows st st.
K 4 rows. Cast off loosely.

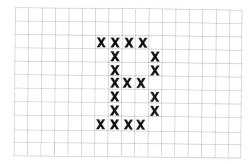

TO MAKE UP
Stitch leg seams to crotch. Stitch front seam from crotch to opening. Lap ends of front bands over each other and stitch sides of bands to cast-off sts at opening. Stitch sleeve seams, leaving 1 cm (1/2 in) open at top for armhole. Stitch sleeves into armhole. Embroider B in duplicate stitch as per graph. Stitch the press studs evenly along the opening. Stitch side and cast-on edges of socks. Thread shirring elastic through first st st row at ankle.

TOWN SUIT FOR FASHION DOLL

MATERIALS
Approx 20 g (1 oz) of 4 ply in red; one pair of 2.75 mm (No. 12) knitting needles; two red buttons; one press stud.

SIZE
To fit any fashion doll approx 30 cm (12 in) in height.

TENSION
26 sts and 36 rows to 10 cm (4 in) over stocking st, using 3 mm (No. 11) Ns.

ABBREVIATIONS
See page 7.

DRESS (main section)
Cast on 48 sts and work as follows:
Row 1: K1, * p2, k2, rep from * to last 3 sts, p2, k1.
Row 2: * P1, * k2, p2, rep from * to last 3 sts, k2, p1.
Rep these 2 rows for patt. Cont in patt until 38 rows worked.
Divide for armholes
Next row: Rib 11, cast off 2, rib 22, cast off 2, rib to end.
Work on these last sts only for left back:
Work 11 rows rib. Cast off.

Rejoin yarn to centre group of sts and work front as follows:
Work 6 rows rib.
Shape neck
Next row: Rib 7, cast off 8, rib 7.
Work on these last 7 sts only for first side:
Work 4 rows rib. Cast off.

Rejoin yarn to rem 7 sts and work 4 rows rib. Cast off.

Rejoin yarn to last group of sts. Work 11 rows rib. Cast off.

SLEEVES (make 2)
Cast on 14 sts and work 32 rows rib

as for dress.
Cast off.

SCARF
Cast on 14 sts and work 88 rows rib as for dress. Cast off.

HANDBAG
Cast on 14 sts and k 26 rows.
Next row: K1, k2tog, k to last 3 sts, k2tog, k1.
Next row: K to end.
Rep last 2 rows four times more. (4 sts.)
Next row: (K2tog) twice.
Next row: K2tog; fasten off.

TO MAKE UP
DRESS
Stitch shoulder seams. Stitch side seams of sleeves and stitch into armholes. Stitch back seam, leaving top 4 cm (1 1/2 in) open. Make two button loops on right side of back opening and sew buttons on left side.

SCARF
Cut 28 x 7-cm (2 3/4-in) pieces of yarn and make a fringe at each end.

HANDBAG
Stitch side seams. Sew a press stud to flap.

TRACKSUIT FOR FASHION DOLL

MATERIALS
Approx 25 g (1 oz) 4 ply in green; a smaller ball of the same yarn in white; one pair each 2.75 mm (No. 12) and 3 mm (No. 11) knitting needles; six press studs; shirring elastic.

SIZE
See page 73.

TENSION
See page 73.

ABBREVIATIONS
See page 7.

TROUSERS (make 2)
Using 2.75 mm (No. 12) Ns and GR, cast on 14 sts; work 4 rows k1, p1 rib.
Next row: * Rib 1, inc in next st, rep from * to end. (21 sts.)
Change to 3 mm (No. 11) Ns and work 10 rows st st.
Cont in st st and inc 1 st at each end of next row and every fol 10th row until 27 sts on N.
Work 13 rows st st, thus ending with WS row.
Cast off 2 sts at beg of next 2 rows.
Dec 1 st at beg of next 4 rows. (19 sts.)
Work 4 rows st st, dec 1 st at centre of last row.
Change to 2.75 mm (No. 12) Ns and work 4 rows k1, p1 rib.
Cast off loosely ribwise.

JACKET (worked in one piece to armholes)
Using 2.75 mm (No. 12) Ns and GR, cast on 40 sts and work 4 rows k1, p1 rib. Change to 3 mm (No. 11) Ns and cont in stripe patt as fols:
Change to W and work 2 rows st st.
Change to GR and work 2 rows st st.
Rep these 4 rows for patt.
Cont in patt until 22 rows completed.
Divide for armholes
Keep stripe pattern correct:
Next row: Patt 9, cast off 2, patt 18,

cast off 2, patt to end. Work on these last sts only for left front.
Work 8 rows patt, thus ending at neck edge.
Shape neck
Next row: Cast off 4 sts, patt to end. (5 sts.)
Work 4 rows patt.
Cast off.

Rejoin yarn to centre group of sts and work for back as fols:
Work 13 rows patt.
Cast off.

Rejoin yarn to rem sts and work to match left front, rev neck shaping.

SLEEVES (make 2)
Using 2.75 mm (No. 12) Ns and GR, cast on 14 sts and work 4 rows k1, p1 rib.
Next row: * Rib 3, inc in next st, rep from * to last 2 sts, rib 2. (18 sts.)
Change to 3 mm (No. 11) Ns and work 28 rows stripe patt.
Cast off.

FRONT BORDER
Using 2.75 mm (No. 12) Ns and GR, pick up and k 24 sts up edge of right front.
Work 3 rows k1, p1 rib.
Cast off loosely ribwise.
Work a border on left front to match.

COLLAR
Using 2.75 mm (No. 12) Ns and GR, cast on 32 sts and work 7 rows k1, p1 rib.
Cast off loosely ribwise.

TOG BAG
SIDE SECTIONS (make 2)
Using 3 mm (No. 11) Ns and W, cast on 7 sts and k 1 row.
Cont in gst and inc 1 st at each end of next row and fol alt row.
K 10 rows.
Dec 1 st at each end of next row and fol alt row. (7 sts.)

K 1 row.
Cast off.

MAIN SECTION
Using 3 mm (No. 11) Ns and GR, cast on 22 sts and k 100 rows.
Cast off.

STRAPS (make 2)
Using 3 mm (No. 11) Ns and W, cast on 32 sts and k 2 rows.
Cast off.

TAB
Using 3 mm (No. 11) Ns and GR, cast on 6 sts and k 16 rows.
Cast off.

TO MAKE UP
JACKET
Stitch shoulder seams. Stitch seams of sleeves and stitch sleeves into armholes. Stitch collar round neck. Space five press studs evenly down front opening.

TROUSERS
Stitch inner leg seams to crotch. Stitch crotch seam. Thread shirring elastic through top and bottom edge of waist ribbing.

TOG BAG
Stitch sides of main section to side sections. Stitch straps in place. Stitch tab to centre of opening. Sew press stud to tab and bag.

PARTY SUIT FOR FASHION DOLL

MATERIALS
Approx 20 g (1 oz) of 4 ply in blue; one pair 3 mm (No. 11) knitting needles; three blue buttons; one fancy button or bead; small piece of elastic for headband.

SIZE
See page 73.

TENSION
See page 73.

ABBREVIATIONS
See page 7.

DRESS
Cast on 84 sts and k 4 rows.
Work 20 rows st st.
Next row: * K2tog, rep from * to end.
Next row: * P2tog, rep from * to end. (21 sts.) Work 2 rows st st.
Next row: K8, inc in next st, k3, inc in next st, k8.
Work 3 rows st st, beg with p row.
Next row: K8, inc in next st, k5, inc in next st, k8. (25 sts.)
Work 7 rows st st, beg with p row.
K 5 rows. Cast off.

STRAPS (make 2)
Cast on 10 sts and k 2 rows.
Cast off.

HAIRBAND
Cast on 20 sts and k 4 rows.
Cast off.

BOW
Cast on 9 sts and k 4 rows.
Cast off.

TO MAKE UP
Stitch back seam of dress to within 2 cm (3/4 in) of waist. Stitch straps to top at back and front. Make three buttonloops on right edge of back opening. Sew buttons on left side to match. Gather centre of bow, stitch bead in place and stitch bow to waist. Stitch elastic to ends of hairband.

LEISURE SUIT FOR FASHION DOLL

MATERIALS
Approx 15 g (1¹/₂ oz) 4 ply in white; one pair each 2.75 mm (No. 12) and 3 mm (No. 11) knitting needles; shirring elastic; one button.

SIZE
See page 73.

TENSION
See page 73.

ABBREVIATIONS
See page 7.

SHORTS (make 2)
Using 3 mm (No. 11) Ns, cast on 30 sts and k 4 rows.

Work 8 rows st st.
Shape crotch
Cont in st st and cast off 3 sts at beg of next 2 rows.
Dec 1 st at beg of next 6 rows.
(18 sts.)
Change to 2.75 mm (No. 12) Ns and work 3 rows k1, p1 rib.
Cast off loosely ribwise.

HALTER TOP
BAND
Using 3 mm (No. 11) Ns,
cast on 28 sts and
k 4 rows.
Cast off.

FRONT SECTION (make 2)
Using 3 mm (No. 11) Ns, cast on 6 sts.
Next row: K2, inc in next 2 sts, k2.

(8 sts.)
K 6 rows.
Dec 1 st at each end of next row and fol alt row.
(4 sts.)
K 8 rows.
Cast off.

TO MAKE UP
SHORTS
Stitch inner leg seams to crotch. Stitch crotch seam. Thread shirring elastic through top and bottom of waist ribbing.

TOP
Stitch cast-on edges of front sections to centre of band. Stitch cast-off edges of fronts tog. Make a button loop on one end of band and sew a button on other end.

LIST OF SUPPLIERS

UNITED KINGDOM

John Lewis Partnership
278–306 Oxford Street
London
Tel: (071) 629 7711

Empress Mills Ltd
Dept CS
Empress Street
Colne
Lancashire
Tel: (0282) 863181

Fuller Knit and Sew
128 Sidwell Street
Exeter
Tel: (0392) 577505

Ollerton Machine Knitting Centre
7 Rufford Avenue
New Ollerton
Newark
Nottingham
Tel: (0623) 860366

Elsie's Wools
Dept MKN
R/O Dinam Park Avenue
Ton Pentre
Rhondda
South Wales
Tel: (0443) 431500

Swanky Knitting and Sewing
120 Lancaster Road
Enfield
Middlesex
Tel: (081) 367 8793

Choice
18 Pickford Lane
Bexleyheath
Kent
Tel: (081) 303 8762

Pamela Bush Designs
Dept 7
29 Whitestiles
Workington
Cumbria
Tel: (0900) 64159

Fluffy Fabrics Ltd
Unit 11
D2 Trading Estate
Castle Road
Eurolink (WB)
Sittingbourne
Kent
Tel: (0795) 478775

Birds — Wools & Crafts
6 Longfellow Road
Worcester Park
Surrey
Tel: (081) 337 8605

AUSTRALIA

Knitters of Australia
625 Hampton Street
Brighton
Victoria 3186
Tel: (03) 593 1433

486 Whitehorse Road
Surrey Hills
Victoria 3127
Tel: (03) 836 9614

The Wool Village
Waverley Gardens Shopping Centre
Cnr Jackson & Police Roads
Victoria 3173
Tel: (03) 546 7973

Craft and Woolly
Unit 3A
443 Scarborough Beach Road
Osbourne Park 6017
Western Australia
Tel: (09) 242 5703

The Craft Cottage
491 Highstreet Road
Mount Waverley 3152
Victoria
Tel: (03) 807 3399

Crossways Wools & Fabrics
37 Crossways Shopping Centre
Subiaco 6008
Western Australia
Tel: (09) 381 4286

NEW ZEALAND

Teddy Time
P O Box 26420
Epsom
Auckland
Tel: 624 1747

Love Me Hug Me Toys
3 Saxon Street
Christchurch
Tel: 381 0476

Hocus Pocus
370 Broadway
Newmarket
Auckland
Tel: 529 0664